COLOR & LIGHT

COLOR & LIGHT

NAVIGATING COLOR MIXING
IN THE MIDST OF AN LED REVOLUTION,
A HANDBOOK FOR LIGHTING DESIGNERS

CLIFTON TAYLOR

QUITE SPECIFIC MEDIA   LOS ANGELES

10 9 8 7 6 5 4 3 2 1

Library of Congress Cataloging-in-Publication Data
Names: Taylor, Clifton, author.
Title: Color & light : navigating color mixing in the midst of an led
revolution, a handbook for lighting designers / by Clifton Taylor.
Other titles: Color and light
Description: Los Angeles : Quite Specific Media, 2019. | Includes
bibliographical references and index.
Identifiers: LCCN 2018038510 | ISBN 9781935247197 (alk. paper)
Subjects: LCSH: Color--Handbooks, manuals, etc. | Stage
lighting--Handbooks, manuals, etc.
Classification: LCC QC496.8 .T39 2019 | DDC 535.6--dc23
LC record available at https://lccn.loc.gov/2018038510

All illustrations are by the author, except where otherwise noted.

Cover design by Wade Lageose
Cover illustration by Clifton Taylor

Quite Specific Media
a division of
Silman-James Press
www.silmanjamespress.com
info@silmanjamespress.com

TO THE MEMORY OF JOHN GLEASON:
DESIGNER, TEACHER, AND MENTOR

CONTENTS

FOREWORD

Clifton Taylor understands color better than any other lighting designer I know. The first time I saw Clifton's revelatory use of light in dance, when I was still in college, I saw performers that appeared to float as if translucent at one moment and seemed fully earthbound the next, dancers who appeared and receded in space as colored light and shadow twisted on and around them.

I could tell that he was doing this through shifting color, but how? It seemed magical to me. After the performance, I walked around the lighting positions and stared at the colored filters, in hopes of gleaning some knowledge. Twenty years later, I continue to be astonished at the sophistication with which Clifton chooses and deploys color palettes in dance, theater, opera, and for music. Having read this wonderful and timely book, I finally have genuine insight into how he's been doing it all these years.

Color can help to tell stories in straightforward ways—it can help us believe that we are on a Paris street on a winter's night, or in a lobster shack in Maine in early fall, or in a forest at midsummer surrounded by supernatural beings. Color can help us shift a space from the present moment to the past; it can take us from reality to fantasy to memory. Color can help us tell emotional stories—adding richness and depth to a memory or character, giving a particular actor a certain glow, or even draining color from the world. Color can harness our imaginations along with text and music and movement to create sadness, excitement, fear. Color can change the physical proportions of space and people, manipulating background and foreground, blurring and heightening spatial boundaries, creating and erasing contrast.

But color in light is hard to use. How we perceive it defies easy explanation; the interactions between our brains, our eyes, and colored light surprise and confound. Many designers are afraid of color—perhaps because color choices are so personal, perhaps because color is so wily, resisting simple rules. Clifton Taylor has been joyfully investigating the science and art of color in light thoroughly and thoughtfully during his 30-year career, and this book reveals much of the thinking that has allowed him to manifest his extraordinary wizardry onstage. He revels in the complexities and surprises that color can bring to our physical environment, and he is able to clearly articulate hard-to-verbalize ideas about light. In this book, Clifton walks us through many tools and techniques with huge generosity, offering us a clear window into his own insights and, perhaps even more importantly, giving us useful templates for thinking about color and light, and excellent tools for experimentation that can be used by any artist or student to explore their own vision of the world.

There are many wonderful books on color out there in the world, mostly written by fine artists and scientists, but very little has been written about color and light from the perspective of the collaborative lighting artist. As I've taught my classes at Princeton and explored color and light with my students, I've offered them essays and articles and occasionally chapters from books, but as far as I know, Clifton's is the first book on color and light written with creative and imaginative appeal that also brings history, science, and practical techniques to bear on contemporary lighting problems. He has offered us a book that can truly help an artist, educator, or student frame and clarify their own creative processes when designing with light.

Clifton and I had the same first guide to this exciting world of color and light. It was Clifton's idea that I apply to study at Tisch School of the Arts at NYU, a suggestion he offered when I met him for the first time in the basement of a large theater, when he was the lighting director of a touring dance company and I was a new electrician assigned to help him prepare the color for a performance. Thanks to Clifton, I too was lucky enough to study with John Gleason, a brilliant lighting designer who had even designed for that genius of atmosphere and emotional tone Tennessee Williams. John had developed his own very sophisticated system for thinking about color and light, a system that now seems ahead of its time.

Unfortunately, John died in 2003 at the age of 62 and never, as far as I know, got these ideas down on paper, although his ideas live on in many generations of working designers. Thankfully for all of us, Clifton has spent 30 years building on what John had to offer, and here he extends John's brilliant thinking about color into the present and future. Clifton and I have both also benefited from the wisdom and mentorship of extraordinary lighting designer Beverly Emmons, whose lectures and master classes on color have thrilled students throughout the country.

This book comes at the perfect moment: Everything we know about using color in light is changing. When Clifton and I were John's students, it was understood that we would plan a coherent color palette for a show, a concert, an event—and then order colored gels to put in front of the lights to create that color palette. If you didn't like the color choices that you'd made, ladders had to be pulled out and crews deployed, and it took quite a bit of time to change your mind.

These days, colors can be changed hundreds of times in a few minutes. We now live in a new world of light—a world of LED technology and of moving lights that can change focus and color at the touch of a button. Even our methods of changing color are new: When we change the color of an LED light source, we are no longer subtracting wavelengths of color by adding a color filter to a white light; we are adding and mixing several different colored LEDs to create the color that we want.

These changes allow us to create magic in exciting new ways, but they have also upended traditional practices and theories of color mixing. Some expert guidance for working artists, students, and educators exploring this brave new world is very welcome. Clifton's book tackles the most contemporary of lighting needs, including technology that is really in its infancy (for example, he offers guidance in creating color paths as you move from one color to another from the same source). As the director of the theater program at Princeton University, I'm a happy convert to all this new equipment, which offers us incredibly fluid possibilities, but until now there hasn't been such a clear guide for us, someone who brings a creative eye to LED color choices that I can share with my students.

When Clifton and I studied with John, he had a red rubber stamp that he used on student (then hand-drawn) light plots when he didn't feel that the thought process was clear enough. The rubber stamp said NOT A CONCEPT. The message was a strong incentive to rigorously investigate and thoroughly test our design ideas and lighting choices. I think that John would have found Clifton's thinking here to be rigorous, generous, and inventive, and that he would have loved to use this book in his class. I can't imagine a more thoughtful, creative, articulate, and generous guide to the world of color and light than Clifton Taylor, and I can't wait to use it with my students.

JANE COX
Lighting Designer and Director of the Program in Theater,
Princeton University
July 17, 2018

ACKNOWLEDGMENTS

Thank you to Pat MacKay for suggesting the book; Jules Fisher and Sonny Sonnenfeld for the creation of the Broadway Lighting Master Classes, which became the forum where the basis of this book could be articulated and refined over many years; and to Beverly Emmons, who invited me to partner with her at the Master Classes over many years and where I was able to develop and organize the kernels of thought for this book.

To Maxine Glorsky, stage manager, mentor, and friend; Karole Armitage, who opened my eyes to the possibilities of new colors; Eve Beglarian, who graciously offered me space and friendship; and Electronic Theatre Controls/ETC, for the use of their equipment, laboratories, and expertise over many years. Edouard Getaz, Megumi Eda, William Isaac, and Alejandro Fajardo for their help, participation, and time in putting together the many illustrations and video clips used throughout the book.

Thank you, Gyreum, the beautiful retreat center in Ireland, where I was able to be quiet long enough to get much of this down on paper; and Peter Vincent, husband and best friend.

Finally, my thanks and appreciation to John Gleason, one of the many wonderful teachers at New York University in the 1980s, who is credited with articulating many of the ideas in this book to me and to his many students and collaborators over a long and successful career. I hope that with this book I am able to carry on his work to others.

INTRODUCTION: EXPLORE AND EXPERIMENT

Think about the following various lighting technologies and how each one can communicate meaning to an audience through its specific quirks of operation and color signature:

- The flicker of a cold fluorescent tube being switched on
- The acid glow of a neon beer sign in the back of a dingy bar
- The warm and soft embrace of a carbon filament Edison-era light bulb, with its snaking amber filament visible through its clear glass bulb
- The unexpected spectral shifts of a mercury vapor streetlight as it powers up on a twilit street
- The long afterglow of fading light after a 5000w tungsten Fresnel is "instantly" blacked out
- The cold white of an HMI light source, with its attention-getting brightness and otherworldly effect of rendering colors differently than a filtered tungsten source by virtue of its particular and unique wavelength signature
- The color-drained hue of a low-pressure sodium vapor lamp at full power—an elusive orange amber floodlight that renders everything in monochrome shades

All of these sources are now *legacy* sources, technologies from the 20th century. They defined the way that the 20th and early 21st centuries looked—both inside and outside the theater. This gives me a sense of pause, because it is through our *collective* under-standing of these sources that we can communicate meaning to an audience about a scene or a situation. The *audience's* inherent understanding of light shifts with the technology, so future lighting technologies will bring their own new associations and new ways for the world to look. We will never run out of visual and lighting elements to mine in our storytelling work.

Incandescent and tungsten lamps have been with us for a long time. Thomas Edison began to commercialize the incandes-cent bulb in the 1880s, and London's Savoy Theatre was the first theater to use electric lighting for the stage, later in that decade. Over the past century or so, the art of lighting design has evolved with the electric dimmable filament lamp housed in a theatrical spotlight (an ellipsoidal reflector spotlight was patented in 1937 by Century Lighting), filtered through colored media—"gels"—as its core tool. Arc lamps in several varieties have long been a part of our toolbox, but the primary lighting device for the stage has been the tungsten filament lamp, housed in a focusable spotlight, filtered through a piece of color media, and connected to a vari-able output dimmer. It has served us well for many years.

The collective stability of lamps, spotlights, dimmers, and filters has been enormously important in the development and expan-sion of the theater lighting industry through the 20th and 21st centuries. Because of it, we have been able to develop a language of lighting that allows us to discuss, teach, learn, and explore something as ethereal and immaterial as *light.*

Additionally, this stability has allowed us to communicate and re-create the essence of a given design through relatively simple paperwork, a set of charts. Today, because of the stability and availability of color media and the relatively standardized designs of theatrical lighting equipment, a lighting design can be implemented almost anywhere in the world, regardless of all the variations in equipment and voltage.

The numbers that designate specific gels concretely communicate ideas about subtle variations in color, and allow us to reproduce those variations on different stages. As we transition to a world without actual color media (actual gels), will gel numbers continue to be learned and internalized by designers and electricians? Imagine our conversations about color when we no longer have a commonly understood color reference such as "Roscolux 80."

This book has been written at a time of expansive technological innovation in lighting. We are in the midst of an LED revolution that is shifting the paradigm of color control from one of filters and *subtractive color mixing* to one of emitters and *additive color mixing*. The use of LED-sourced luminaires is now firmly in place, and one's ability to manipulate lighting color in the theater, as well as in our homes and places of business, is rapidly increasing, with weekly announcements of new lighting sources and control systems.

The wholesale adoption of LED technology is changing everything. In the rapidly approaching fully LED world, our conversations will be very different than they are now. Additive color-mixing fixtures using LEDs demand new ways of thinking and new methodologies and pose new challenges in communicating and maintaining a design intent. I'm incredibly optimistic about the potential of LED technology and the flexibility that it offers us as designers to make new choices in color palettes and intensities, such as cues that subtly shift the color of a scene over a period of time or instantaneously accommodate the costume colors of a new character who enters a scene.

It is an exciting time in the world of color and light. New pieces of equipment, precisely engineered to satisfy our specific needs, are coming out at an unprecedented pace. On the software side, we are gaining a new level of control over our equipment, helping us make lighting decisions quickly and reliably. But that is not to say that we have reached a stable or acceptable state. Many things will change in the coming years.

Slower to change, though, is the way that we see color and light, and the more we learn about it, the better we will be able to use it to enhance our work.

Through all the aforementioned technological changes there remains the natural language of color that artists have used for much longer than there has been electric light, a language that we will talk about in this book: more saturated versus less saturated, warmer versus cooler, more green versus more magenta, receding (recessive) versus advancing (dominant). These words and phrases are the bedrock language of color manipulation, whether putting a paintbrush to canvas or calling up color attributes on a modern lighting console.

Color is fundamental to our experience of the world, but the use of color in art and design, especially directly in light, often defies easy explanation. I find that choices of colors and color palettes are among the hardest things to talk about, and I know I'm not alone in this. Our feelings about color reside in a protected corner of our minds. That corner is often not quite logical but rather wrapped up in emotions and feelings, memories and imaginings, and especially culture and poetry. This is a good thing; it is something to be celebrated and nurtured. The connections and resonances that color holds in our mind are not always visual. For me, color is deeply connected to music, and to smell and touch. I cannot always explain *why* I make a certain color choice in my work; I believe that my choices are sometimes made in a part of my brain that is emotional, and perhaps pre-logical.

My sense of color preferences arises from my experience of the world. For any artist or designer, in or out of the theater, experience and observation are the nourishment that brings forth gestural clarity and refined visual communication.

Intuition is also central to the work of anyone involved in creative activities. Our intuition about color helps to define who we are as individual artists and designers, and it should be respected, nurtured, and protected in all that we do. Intuition arises from our unique histories and memories. It flows from the deep well of consciousness itself. For reasons that I cannot fully explain, I find an irreverent pleasure in dabbing some chromium orange into a field of cobalt blue.

I find joy in color—in the relationships of the bright hues in a wildflower, the showy ambers and pinks and lavenders of a summer sunset, the march of silver-white clouds across a chalky blue sky on a clear winter morning. It is the memory of moments like these that I draw upon in my work as a theatrical designer.

Aside from its manifestations in nature, color is deeply connected to the history of all cultures. One could study the history of color in a societal group from several different points of view: the geography of a society and the natural colors in its particular landscape; the technological history of the production of colors, including the relative cost and rarity of certain colors and how they were used in art; and the linguistic history of color names—to name just three.

Our ability to manipulate color through light also has a history that is connected to technologies and industries far away from the worlds of art and theater. This book will touch on these subjects but remain concentrated on how lighting color works in a mixed-media three-dimensional space.

The perception of color involves physics and the physiology of the eye and brain, as well as our psychological and cultural frameworks. The perception of color is relative. The intensity, hue, and saturation of a color will change depending on its surrounding colors. Its qualities will be shifted by comparison with the other colors with which it appears. This book describes one lighting designer's journey to try and understand some of those complexities from a personal point of view.

SCIENCE AND ART

Color as we experience it exists in our brains as a mental construct based on data collected by specialized cells in our eyes that have evolved to detect a narrow band of wavelengths of photonic energy. Photons of a specific range of energy levels are emitted by a source. These photons either bounce off or are absorbed by physical objects.

The bounced ones that happen to enter our eyes are then focused through a lens onto a group of specialized cells in our retina. This in turn generates various chemical responses that then trigger an electrical response in our optic nerve. The electrical signal is transmitted from the eyes to the brain, where a synaptic response occurs. Finally, we perceive that synaptic response as a sensation of color. If that isn't complicated enough, each of us has an individual ideation of color based on individual preferences and cultural biases: subjects of psychology, philosophy, anthropology, and even morality and religion.

Even though these responses are individual, there are some similarities to the common experiencing of color. The fact that we can talk about a color *green* is an indication of this. And while actual perception of a specific color within a palette of colors may differ from person to person, I believe a color's function *within that palette* can be more easily understood in common. In other words, through contrast, harmony, or dissonance, a color can take on a meaning within a specific context.

This is *not* a book on the science of color, though we will touch on some research and scientifically derived information. It *is* a book of experimentation and exploration, written for artists and designers who use light in their work. The result of my personal search for a language of color and light, it is written at a unique moment in the history of lighting technology when we have unprecedented control over light—color, shape, and intensity—in our compositions and designs.

Color is a difficult subject to discuss for all artists. Translating our very personal visual observations and aspirations into words can sometimes collapse subtleties and misstate our true intentions. The use of color in great art will always, to some extent, defy rational analysis, for observation is entangled not only in perception but also in the spheres of feelings and emotion.

In some ways, color can be the most confusing of the tools in the lighting designer's kit. Equipment, angle, intensity, and atmosphere are all more rational and easier to discuss. Color is more difficult. Why should one choose a certain tint of pale blue-green over another? Should the sunlight through the window be yellow or pink or steely blue? There are no general answers to such questions. The designers who are collaborating on a work can only hope to find specific solutions that work in the moment to transmit an idea in the clearest possible manner.

The experience of color, like taste and touch, is one of the great joys of being alive. Revel in its use, make bold choices and don't be afraid of it. Strive for beauty and precision, and be fearless in your experiments.

HOW TO USE THIS BOOK

Color & Light visits our recent past work in subtractive color mixing and introduces techniques to transition to the new world of additive color mixing. My hope is that the structure of its chapters will form a series of tutorials that can serve as reminder and review of where we have come from and a guide to how we can move ahead.

The book may be approached in several ways: as the basis for a course on color for visual artists who work with light, explored individually or collectively in a classroom setting, or individual chapters on specific subjects may be used as a reference guide when thinking about certain color problems. It includes discussions of natural, tungsten, arc, as well as LED sources, each of which presents its own set of issues, challenges, and opportunities for the lighting designer. The principals of manipulating color are germane to each of the source types, and the techniques that you learn for tungsten sources will translate to arc sources and to LED luminaires.

You will gain a greater understanding of the concepts and exercises outlined in this book if you have access to a well-equipped lighting laboratory. This lab would consist of a room with various types of lighting equipment (of theatrical and non-theatrical provenance), a full range of color filters, available power, and dimmers, and, importantly, realistic mannequins and access to a range of clothing and fabrics to see under light. It is also important to paint one of the walls of this lab a flat (matte) base white, to act as a cyclorama or sky backdrop. (See Appendix A for a proposed light lab design and a list of proposed equipment.)

As with all aspects of visual art, it's essential that you see and experience for yourself the concepts being discussed. No words on a page, no app or computer simulation can substitute for the experience of seeing the effects of lighting color with your own eyes.

This book is intended to help you discover your own answers to questions of "Which color?" by helping to define all the aspects of a color that might be separately considered. While those answers will always be personal and artistic choices, I hope that this book will guide you toward making them in ways that communicate your feelings and storytelling goals most effectively.

The subject of light is important to anyone who works with color in any media. We experience color *only* through the medium of light. We experience the blueness of a section of paint or the goldenness of a piece of silk only when these surfaces reflect light into our eyes. Light *is* color, and therefore this book is relevant for all visual artists who work with color in any media.

It is impossible in the 21st century for a work on color to avoid the subject's connections to various scientific disciplines, and I've attempted to outline the basic physical, biological, linguistic, engineering, and psychological components of current color studies in a way that is clear and readable for a non-scientific audience. That said, Chapters 2 and 3 (What Is Color? and Primary Colors in Light) deal most heavily with the scientific aspects of color and can be skipped without losing the thread of the discussion.

1.

WHY COLOR?

OVERVIEW

Consider five important properties of light: angle, shape, intensity, change-through-time, and color. What is unique about color
among these properties? What can color do that other variables
within our control cannot do?

Since colored light exists in nature, we may choose to use color
when it's necessary to accurately portray real lighting in our work
within a lit space.

Imagine this scene for a stage set:

*A room in Malibu, California, in the late afternoon. A large
window faces the sea. There is a woman in a chair reading a
book. The chair is near the window, but the woman has turned
on a lamp so that she can better see what she is reading. Behind
her, there is a doorway that leads out to a room where a man is
working at a counter. Above him, an overhead fluorescent light
is illuminated.*

Think about the three sources of light described. Each has
its own qualities of diffusion, brightness, angle, and color.
Concentrate on the color of these three sources: the late afternoon sunlight, the reading light, and the fluorescent light in the

other room. If you were re-creating this scene for a stage, you might choose color filters for the stage lights to mimic these real sources. Instead of filtered stage lights, you might also choose different types of lights, with different intrinsic color properties, to actually be or to enhance the sources of light in the scene.

When I choose color for a project, especially for a play that is based in reality, I start by finding out what the colors realistically might be. If I am using tungsten stage lights to substitute for all three sources, my next task would be to search for filters that would best simulate the story of these three lighting sources.

- What colors might be in an afternoon sunlight in Malibu?
- What about the incandescent reading light? That is the source that is most like an unfiltered tungsten stage light.
- What about the fluorescent light? Can its color be reproduced with incandescent stage lights?

So even in this seemingly simple setup, the color of the light is an important consideration in rendering the realism of the scene. But now think about some additional parameters: What is the context of the scene? Is it the opening scene in a play, or a scene from a musical comedy, or the end of a tragic opera? Would the context of the scene change how you might render the color of the three lighting sources? Would the colors of the costumes or the colors of the walls change how you might choose the colors for the three sources of light? Finally, would either the scale of the stage set or the scale of the theater itself change the colors of the light in the scene?

To answer these questions, consider that there are four roles that color could play in any lighting design:

- for storytelling
- for style
- in the service of scenery, costume, and other color choices in the total visual work, such as projections, or the hair color of a particular performer
- as a tool for rendering spatial dimension

Each of these four components of a color choice may be considered in conjunction with other lighting choices, such as angle or intensity, but they can always also be considered in terms of color alone.

STORYTELLING

Everyone who creatively participates in the process of making theater is a storyteller. Each of us—playwright, actor, director, choreographer, composer, and designer—contributes to the storytelling event of a production. As lighting designers, scene descriptions like the one in Malibu form the basis of our story-telling contribution.

We don't know the nature of the relationship between the man and the woman from this description, but we do know that they exist in separate environments that are lit very differently. That is the kind of story that a lighting designer can tell. We can render environments that the audience can read as realistically sourced by natural light or artificial light. We can communicate time of day and qualities of weather and season through light. Color is a major component of our toolbox to tell these kinds of stories.

COMMUNICATING STYLE

Here are some questions that one could ask to help understand the connection of lighting to style:

- What kind of show is happening in that Malibu house?
- Can the color of the light communicate something about the style of the event that we're watching?
- Is it helpful to this particular theatrical event for the color of the light to take on that job?

Here's an example: Perhaps the woman in the scene must make a choice between the man in the workroom and the freedom that is represented by the window. I can imagine several roles for color within a scene like this. One possibility is that the afternoon sunlight takes on a deeply saturated orange hue, while the fluorescent light from the workroom casts a harsh greenish light that is almost ghostly. The light cast from the reading lamp becomes the neutral source, or a reference white. By pushing the contrast between the amber of the sunlight and the green of the fluorescent, the lighting designer could create a visual environment that embodies the psychological state of the woman who must make this choice. A lighting environment that visually manifests her choice through these contrasting colors leads us to the question of style. Because style answers the question of how much contrast is correct, increasing the contrast in the colorations of the scene, i.e., increasing the saturation, could abstract the idea. Ideally, by finding the right level of abstraction through choosing the colors, the lighting designer connects an audience to the overall stylistic intent of the production: the writing, the acting, and direction of the entire work.

A very beautiful example of this was Christopher Akerlind's lighting design for the musical The Light in the Piazza *(for which he won both a Tony Award and a Drama Desk Award). His use of buttery warm light to express the hyper-romantic world of 1950s Florence connected the audience to a collective memory of postwar Italy. The color of the lighting, in concert with angle and cueing choices, created a dreamy and filtered version of Italy that very beautifully communicated both the filters through which the main character experienced the world and the filters of language and culture that were being bridged in the show. The warm softness of Akerlind's colors communicated the fragile innocence of the time, the characters, and the place.*

Style is not only a function of color choice, but color is always a part of the style of a lighting design.

IN SERVICE OF PERFORMERS, SCENERY, AND COSTUMES

Would the specific colors of the scenery or the costumes of the characters affect the choices of color in the lighting?

Lighting color choices are usually influenced by the local colors of the scenery and costumes. Sometimes the hair color or special makeup of a lead performer will influence the lighting color choices. Imagine choices for lighting color that would support the central room in the Malibu example. Now imagine that the woman is to be wearing a green dress while sitting in a royal blue chair. Knowing this, perhaps one would choose a version of incandescent white that is made slightly cooler or bluer to work with the decor and costume.

Now imagine that the actor is to be dressed in pink while sitting on a chair with oranges and magentas in its patterned fabric. Can you see how this decision might alter the choice for lighting color? Each visual design element—scenery, costume, projection, and lighting—is telling a story with color. It is not only possible but necessary that the color of the light be tuned so that everything works together to realize the potential of all of the colors used in a scene. This work does not reduce the importance of the lighting story, but like players in an orchestra, each design element contributes part of a complete event that ideally is the result of all the individual choices.

About the evolution of colored light.

Colored transparent or translucent filters for stage lighting predate even the electric lamp. Prior to electric lighting, candle-light and gaslight were filtered through colored silks, colored water, even wine. Later gelatin, then high-heat plastics, and finally metal-coated dichroic glass were developed and marketed with de-facto-standardized numbering systems.

The filters that we now use have had an unprecedented stability over decades of worldwide use, so much so that the trade name numbers of many of the filters have become the common way of speaking about color among lighting professionals.

Brigham colored transparent gelatin sheets were brought to market in the 1870s. Plastics, introduced after World War II, could better withstand the heat of stage lights. Importantly, the method of choosing colors from a swatch book of color filters in one's studio has remained consistent for almost 150 years.

Adding further stability, the majority of Lee brand filters in the 100 series gained their numbers from Cinemoid numbers that were introduced in the 1960s by Strand. We've had over 50 years of stable numbering in color filters, and generations of designers and technicians and programmers have memorized and internalized these numbers. The industry understands a common language of color because of these numbering systems.

RENDERING SPACE

Stage space has qualities of magic. It is a changeling that has the ability to mutate from safe to dangerous, from quotidian to profound, from infinitesimal to infinite, all with the shift of a line or a lighting cue. But if the space has magical properties, it is because we, the theater makers, are the magicians. Like gravity, magic is a force unseen without an object or a person upon which to act. The composers and writers pen the words that are spoken and the songs that are sung, but it is the designers whose job it is to create the illusion of space through cloth and paint and light. Color is vital to this endeavor.

Think of the window in our Malibu scene. What are the colors of the sky, what are the colors of the Pacific Ocean? How can color help the illusion that a backdrop is an ocean and sky of immense proportion and depth? Perhaps, in reality, this backdrop is only a few inches away from the window. Are there colors that you could pick that would make the image of the sky recede and let the light around the actress dominate the scene? This book will explore the possibility that our sense of color and our sense of depth are closely related. For now, think about this possibility and try and imagine colors that might give a sense of depth or that recede in a composition, and colors that might push forward or flatten an apparent perception of depth in a composition.

CONCLUSION

When thinking about color in light, ask yourself these questions:

- Can the color of the light communicate a story point, perhaps by realistically indicating a time of day or a realistic source of light to an audience?
- What is the style of the event: Is it realistic, farcical, romantic, naturalistic, or something else? What kinds of colors, specifically lighting colors, could best communicate that style to an audience? Is there some historical research that one could find to help in discussions with collaborators about this style? What is happening with the stylistic use of color in the other designs?
- Is the lighting color serving to unify a collective visual statement that includes the color palettes of the scenery and costumes?
- Is there a way to better use color to enhance the intended spatial dimensions of the stage, either by increasing or decreasing the apparent sense of depth in a scene?

Answering these questions will lead you to a solution for choosing colors for the light in your scene. The intent of this book is to give you techniques and greater understanding of color in order to answer these questions in your own way.

Tip: Look for ways to use contrast in your work to enhance dimensionality, depth, and richness in your compositions.

PRACTICAL: CREATE A SIMPLE LIGHTING AND GROUND PLAN BASED ON THE DESCRIPTION OF THE MALIBU SCENE

1. In a schematic way, draw a plan on a piece of paper based on the description of the house in Malibu as it would be in reality. Show the placement and colors of all the light sources necessary to realize the description. Do not worry about simulating the described light, but rather first draw the ground plan of the rooms and the lighting as described.

2. On a separate piece of paper, modify the room so that it could work for a scene on a proscenium stage. Then add in the location and colors of lighting instruments that might be used to support the realistic scene on a stage. With the knowledge that you now have, be as specific as possible about your instrument choices and color choices.

2.

WHAT IS COLOR?

PHOTONS AND WAVELENGTH

In the world of objects, we think of color as being a property of something. A dab of paint has a color. We paint the table blue; we dye the carpet red. With objects, color is something that can be applied to a surface or dyed into the material. Color can also be an intrinsic property of something, as in "the wood is brown." The brownness of the wood is one of its many properties.

Before the widespread use of LED sources, in order to achieve a specific color of light, we usually filtered a white light source, using some kind of physical barrier, to take away the unwanted wavelengths and arrive at a desired color. Because we were working mostly with white light sources, we came to think of color as being somehow separate from the light, a choice that was in a different column from intensity or lamp type in our spreadsheets and specifications.

Full-color-mixing LED sources reveal this way of thinking about color to have limitations. These types of fixtures have no "default" white light. There is no such thing as "No Color" or "Open White," terms that lighting designers have commonly used that have no intrinsic meaning with regard to these fixtures. What we are left with is the reminder (or perhaps realization) that all versions of "white" light are mixtures of component colors of light.

So, what makes these colors of light? When an electron changes its state (from one energy level to another), it is possible that the atom to which it is bound can emit a photon. The photon leaves the confines of the atom and vibrates at a measurable frequency. Depending on that frequency, when the photon encounters another atom, the photon will either be bounced or absorbed. We have evolved a system to measure the wavelength of that photon, so that if it enters into our eye, most of us know with pretty good accuracy what the very specific wavelength of that photon was and also where it came from in our visual field. That is a lot of data to process! Our brains have evolved to process this information in an elegant way. We experience discrete wavelengths of photons as colors. Color is a brain construct that has evolved to deal with the experience of different energy levels of a stream of photons.

When a photon hits our retina, it causes an electro-chemical response that, depending on the exact signature of that response, causes our brain to perceive a color at that location in our retinal array. By analyzing the full array of responses, our brain creates a picture of reality based upon the subtle differences in wavelengths of the photons stimulating our retinas. The experience of color is thus created in our brains.

Our vision system processes only a very small subset of all the photons that it may encounter. All visible light and all the colors of the spectrum fall into a narrow band of energy levels—photons whose wavelengths fall into a range between 390 and 700 nano-meters. Photons that fall outside of this energy range are radio and television waves, ultraviolet waves, X-rays, gamma rays, etc.

But why did our vision system evolve to only see this narrow band? The answer has to do with this specific planet, with its very particular atmosphere. The atmosphere acts as a blanket around the earth and absorbs photons from large ranges of the full spectrum. Photons between 390nM and 700nM comprise one range of energy that is not blocked, not absorbed, by our atmosphere; but millions of years of evolution provided a way to use the available range of photonic energy to be able to see.

One can imagine that life on a different planet, with a different sun and a different atmosphere, might evolve a vision system perhaps having no relationship to how we humans experience color here on Earth.

Illus. 2.1.

In most natural forms of light—sunlight, moonlight, or firelight—billions of distinct frequencies mix together to make what we call "white light." White light is a mix of photons vibrating at different frequencies covering the range of the visible spectrum.

"Local color," as it applies to objects that we perceive as colored—paint, dye, and pigment—refers to a property of matter whereby an atom within a molecule will absorb or reflect photons depending on the photon's specific wavelength. When we observe an object reflecting photons of a certain wavelength, we observe that the object has a color.

For an object to appear to be of a certain color, photons (vibrating at a frequency that corresponds to that color) are reflected off the object into our eyes and onto our retinas. In other words, for us to see that an object has a color, it is because that color is present in the light that is reflected from the object into our eyes.

When we experience that a leaf is green, what has happened is that the leaf has absorbed most of the red and blue wavelengths of light and reflects most of the green wavelengths. Plants do not use green light to carry out photosynthesis, they need red and blue light. Since the green light is reflected by the atoms that make up the leaf, but the blue and red light is absorbed, we perceive the leaf as being green.

VISIBLE SPECTRUM

Illus. 2.2.

Since the mathematical work of James Clerk Maxwell in the late 1800s on electromagnetic fields, we have known that the visible spectrum is a small slice of a much larger range of electromagnetic radiation. Our human eyes and brains process, i.e., see, these particular wavelengths as visible light. At the low end of the spectrum, at around 390nM, ultraviolet colors transition into indigo/blue and become detectable by our eyes. At a point beyond 700nM, red light transitions into infrared and the electromagnetic radiation that we call light ceases to be visible.

The full range of electromagnetic radiation is much larger than the slice that we see as light and color. It includes radio and television signals, microwaves, X-rays, and gamma rays. The elementary particle involved in all of these waves is the photon.

Our eyes have evolved to respond to photons vibrating within a narrow range of wavelengths that hit our retina. Other animals have eyes that respond to different ranges of wavelengths; they respond differently to the same input of wavelengths and therefore see color quite differently than we do. For instance, dogs' and cats' eyes do not respond specifically to red colors; they have color detectors in their retinas for blue and green ranges, but not red.

The specific range of radiation that we perceive as visual light corresponds closely to a window of energy levels that our atmosphere does not absorb on its way from the sun to the earth. Our atmosphere absorbs most of the ultraviolet radiation and most of the infrared spectrum that fall upon it. Our visual systems have evolved to detect and perceive the light that is not absorbed by, but which passes through, our atmosphere. This range is called the "optical window."

Our brain aggregates the data from roughly 4.5 million cone cells in each of our two eyes into an experience that, if the energy of the light is such, we may call "green." Light green or dark green depends on further analysis from the response of the 90 million rod cells in each of our two eyes.

The cells are arranged on the back surface of our eye (the retina) and respond to light that has been focused onto them by a lens. The arrangement and distribution of the various types of cells is unique to each person, much like a fingerprint.

IT'S ALL IN YOUR HEAD

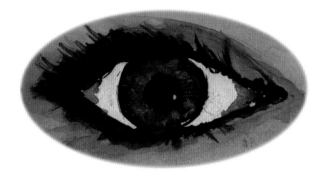

Illus. 2.3.

When a cell in the retina absorbs a photon, it produces a chemical reaction. This chemical reaction is translated into an electrical response by the optic nerve. The brain analyzes the specific electrical response of the optic nerve and creates a concept of color. This is an important insight. Color as we know it exists only in our brains.

Blueness results from the brain's interpretation of an event in which photons with wavelengths of around 450nM hit the retina. Color is an evolutionary result of a biological response to the existence of photonic energy or particles.

COLOR AND CULTURE

Like all things that take place inside our heads, we have an individual response to the colors that we experience. This response, this individual experience of color, is shaped and refined by both the cultural and natural environments within which we reside. While all human beings share a similar vision system, color is interpreted and prioritized in ways that are affected by collective experiences. We can see this when looking at the vocabulary that different languages use to describe colors.

Many premodern languages didn't distinguish between the colors blue and green. Until the modern era, there was no separate word for those two hues in Mandarin. If there isn't a word to describe a color, would a speaker of that language share an understanding of the possible meanings of that color in a work of art with someone from a culture whose language distinguishes the two hues?

It's a difficult question to test, but I believe that the linguistic history shows that one's understanding of color is at least in part culturally based. This theory makes certain kinds of storytelling more difficult, but in my opinion, this is not a bad thing. It means that we cannot expect an audience to come to our work with preconceived notions of any kind of intrinsic color meanings. Blue has no more absolute meaning than does yellow. A musical analogy (I love musical analogies to light) would be that the note D♯ has no intrinsic meaning but could acquire meaning within the context of a specific musical composition. In the same way, yellow does not have a universal meaning, but it could acquire a meaning within the context of a visual composition.

This linguistically inspired insight, that our understanding of color is connected to culture, yields an important possibility. Because the use of color is an expression of culture and can be tied to periods of time, technology, and a local natural environment, color itself can be a subject of cultural research.

This is important because that research points us to a way of making color choices that are specific to an event, that move beyond our own personal responses. The color of sunlight hasn't changed since the 1940s, but the use of Technicolor film stock in that decade alters our collective memory of colors from that period and provides a possible reason to choose a specific kind of color for sunlight for a project set in that decade.

CULTURAL EVOLUTION

Illus. 2.4. A hierarchy of colors.

In *Basic Color Terms: Their Universality and Evolution*, the authors, Brent Berlin and Paul Kay, describe their 1969 study that discovered a hierarchy of basic color terms across languages. Based on a survey of the color terms in many spoken languages, they found that color words evolve with the development of language in a standard order, starting with black and white, then adding red, then yellow or green.

After that point, the order of color word development begins to break down, but the process often follows this sequence:

1. black and white
2. red
3. either green or yellow
4. both green and yellow

5. blue
6. brown
7. purple, pink, orange, or gray

The shared list of basic color terms across languages is very limited. And even within a language the number of universally understood color terms is small. For instance, by a set of rigorous linguistic rules, the English language has 11 universal basic color terms in wide usage: black, white, red, green, yellow, blue, brown, orange, pink, purple, and gray. This makes color naming in lighting, paint, and fashion somewhat arbitrary.

Illus. 2.5. The English language hierarchy of universal colors.

WHY DO WE NEED SO MANY COLORS?

If there are only these 11 basic universal terms, why do we need hundreds of possible gel filter color choices or a million theoretical choices on a color-mixing luminaire? The devil is, as usual, in the details. We may have an instinct that a light should be pale blue, but the choice of which pale blue may well be based on the costume color of the lead dancer, the colors of the lights in other areas of the composition, the angle of the pale blue light in relation to the viewers, or the intensity level of the source luminaire.

All of these considerations may help one decide whether the light should be colored with Lee 201, Roscolux 61, or Apollo 4800 (three manufacturer-specific names of different pale blue filters), or whether the pale blue emitter is set to 67.74% or 72.46%. While all the resulting colors could be called pale blue, each is composed of a slightly different recipe of colors, and each will output a different spectral curve. A color choice for an artistic composition often begins with a guess, a feeling, or an intuition. This is true whether working with color filter media or with an LED color-mixing luminaire.

Start with your instinct for what a color should be. All of the other choices that vibrate around your initial choice are there to help solve possible problems that may arise. As an example, say you want to use a pale blue to light a singer. When you turn the light on, you think that perhaps your initial choice of Roscolux 61 has too much green for the singer's skin tone. The light can still be pale blue, but perhaps instead of Roscolux 61, choose another pale blue color with less green and more red in it.

CONCLUSION

It is impossible to have light without color. All visible light is color. The colors that we see are based upon a biological process. These perceptions are further influenced by culture and language. Even within a culture, color is not necessarily a universal, objective experience. It is rather a subjective experience that one individual cannot be sure is exactly shared by another. For this reason, color preferences by an individual artist or designer are subjective and open to interpretation. That is different from saying that there are no shared understandings of color palettes. In many cultures, the use of color is highly regimented by norms in costume, painting, and decor. The existence of these cultural color palettes can help shape and inform a lighting palette that might work for a given situation.

> **Tip:** *One of the most important lessons that I ever learned (and continue to learn) was an instruction to "see with my eyes." I think this statement means to tell us not to expect or anticipate what we will see, but to let ourselves actually experience each visual moment, each scene, before us. Give yourself to the experience of deeply seeing. Don't believe you know a work of art because you've seen a reproduction in a book. If you can, go and experience the actual work. Do the same thing with the natural world: Seek out and look at the colors in the evening sky, study the shadows that appear in a wooded glen. See with your eyes!*

PRACTICAL: COLOR RESEARCH

A color in itself has no intrinsic or commonly agreed-upon meaning. We might say that red is the color of blood, but it is also the color of apples. Red alone, outside of any context, cannot equal blood. Nor can red light easily symbolize blood, since there is no realistic common experience of white light becoming red through a blood filter.

It is dangerous to assume that your personal association with a color will translate to a viewer without an explanation or strong contextual backing. Similarly, it must be observed that we, when considered across human cultures, do not agree on a universal meaning for light that is blue. It is only in a specific utilization, within the context of a story, a production, or a particular design, that a color or group of colors might possibly take on an articulated meaning beyond "what light through yonder window breaks." *Context may give color meaning, but color that is disconnected from context cannot have a generally understood meaning.*

If a plausible context can be provided, however, it is possible to design color palettes where meaning is felt or intellectually understood by an audience. A cool glow of moonlight and a soft beam of warm lamplight that breaks through an upper window onto the balcony can tell us that Juliet is there, waiting. Here, the color of those two sources can take on meaning because of how they reference a real world of moonlight and lamplight of a Verona night. An audience will have a feeling for these color relationships based on their own experiences and, at least subconsciously, use their own knowledge to evaluate the truthfulness of these choices.

Color research involves actively seeing and remembering the color of light in different situations. It also involves collecting, remembering, and sharing examples of how others have used color in their visual compositions.

EXERCISE

Create and maintain a set of files of pictures that show color and light. Categorize your collection in terms of color, subject, and period style. Broaden your quest for research materials beyond the Internet and work that can be displayed on a screen. Magazines and postcards are good places to start. We are surrounded by imagery! Be a collector of colors and color palettes that are unusual, beautiful, evocative, dissonant, harsh, smooth, and emotional. Use those files when thinking about color for a performance work. Share your research with your collaborators as a way of talking about color, but be careful: Color in one format is not always easily translated to another. When you use research with your collaborators, be as clear as possible about how the research fits into the project's overall goals.

Lighting color research does not have to be limited to realistic paintings or photographs. Inspiration can be found in many places. Look at color in different media and notice how it is different and how it is the same. Color on fabric versus shiny paper. Colored light versus colored objects. Over time, your research library will develop into a tool that you can use to help you make choices when filling out a color palette.

Find images where a particular color is prominent and see how the other colors in the image support that prominence. File those images under the prominent color.

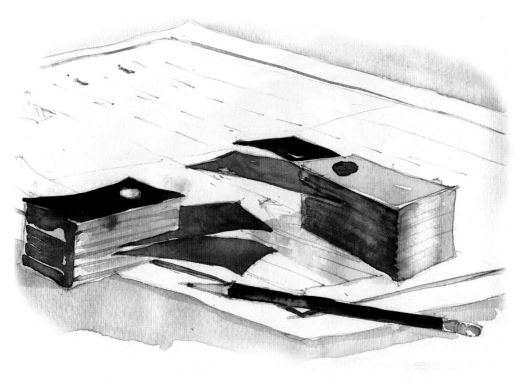

Illus. 2.6. Choosing color from swatch books.

3.

PRIMARY COLORS IN LIGHT

Sir Isaac Newton, working around the turn of the 18th century in England, experimented with refracted light.

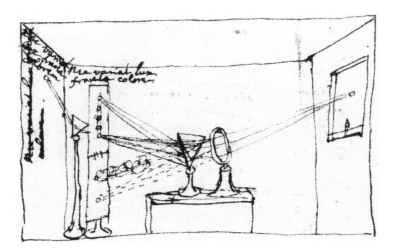

Illus. 3.1. Sir Isaac Newton's illustration of his refraction experiment, in which sunlight was refracted through a prism.

He wrote that there are seven colors in refracted light: red, orange, yellow, green, blue, indigo, and violet, and published a book entitled *Opticks* about his findings. Newton perceived seven bands of color, but I earlier stated that sunlight was composed of a continuous range of frequency bandwidths. How is this reduced to just seven colors?

Spectral colors coming from sunlight do in fact form a continuous band of frequencies. In this band of frequencies, or colors, no frequency of light is inherently more important than any other frequency. Sunlight is emitted across the entire frequency range.

When this sunlight is subjected to refraction and we can see its component parts, as in a rainbow after a storm or through a glass prism like Newton used, we are presented with a continuous spectrum of colored light. Something strange happens when we look at this spectrum, though. We often think of a rainbow as having a set of color bands. Perhaps these bands blend together or have soft edges, but when most people look at a rainbow they see it as being made up of distinct bands of colored light. No such color striping actually exists in the refracted light itself. Our brains take this almost infinitely scalable range of color and reduce it to a nameable set of seven color stripes. The striping, the reduction of a continuous range of color into apparently discrete sections, is a result of data overload: a way that our brains make this information practical.

CONES IN OUR EYES MAKE PRIMARY COLORS

Think of an analog radio tuner for a moment. As you turn the dial, moving the needle up and down the frequency spectrum, stations come into and out of focus. When the frequency is set to a number near a transmitting radio signal, you may hear the station, but it has static and may not be very clear.

Our eyes work in a similar way, only instead of one tuner dial we have three types of tuners in our eyes, and each one of these tuner types (called *cone cells*) is tuned to a different range of frequencies. We interpolate the data from these three types of cells to be able to detect all the variations in color across the spectrum. The banded appearance of the rainbow is a result of the interpolation process where we favor, because of our evolution, certain ranges of light wavelengths.

WE ARE TRICHROMATS

The surface of our retinas is covered with specialized cells that chemically respond to a limited range of light wavelengths. The three types of cone cells detect wavelengths near 570nM (these are called "L" cone cells, for long wavelengths), 540nM ("M" cone cells, for medium wavelengths), and 430nM ("S" cone cells, for short wavelengths). These three wavelengths correspond loosely to the colors red (L), green (M), and blue (S). Each of these cells responds, or tunes in to, a range of wavelengths, with the peak response near the given values.

The brain, receiving data for each area of vision from at least three of these cells (usually many more), makes choices about the color that it is seeing by weighing the relative level of stimulation of the three types of cells. So, if a few thousand photons of light hit your retina at a certain spot and the L cones (red) in the area really respond, the nearby M cones (green) also respond but not as much, and the S cones not at all, your brain will conjure up an image of orange. Think about the huge amount of processing and calculation this takes for everything you look at. It's amazing, isn't it?

Because we only have these three types of detection cells to differentiate all the colors that we can see (thought to number around one million distinct colors), it follows that all the other colors must be derived from these three. Sir Isaac Newton had this insight even without knowing anything about the structure of our eyes or brains. He saw that one could create a version of all of the spectral colors through variably mixing these three particular colors. We name these colors "primary."

After Newton, it was over 200 years before we began to understand why three colors are primary and why these colors are different depending on whether we are talking about light or pigments.

In printer inks, the three primary colors are cyan, magenta, and yellow. This is because pigments, like lighting filters, are subtractive color-mixing systems. One starts with a white paper and applies an ink to remove wavelengths of light from being reflected. Magenta ink works by absorbing green *wavelengths of light and reflecting* blue *and* red *wavelengths. Similarly, yellow ink works by absorbing* blue *wavelengths and reflecting* green *and* red *wavelengths. By mixing magenta and yellow inks, one can arrive at a red hue, which is a true primary color of light.*

Except for the way our eyes and brains have evolved to perceive things, there is nothing in nature that is necessarily special about red, green, or blue. They exist as primary colors for us because of the evolution of the human eye.

When our eyes see light that has the frequency that we call cyan, the blue cones and the green cones are stimulated to levels that we identify as cyan. Strangely though, without projecting any light that has the frequency of cyan light, but replacing it with a mixture of primary blue light and primary green light that stimulates our eyes in the same way as the cyan frequency does, we can trick our brains into thinking that we are seeing cyan. That is how additive color mixing works, where we add two colors of light coming from the same angle onto the same surface.

In the human vision system, to continue my earlier radio-dial analogy, we can never tune directly into the cyan radio station. We who have never experienced the cyan radio station only know that it is somewhere in the static between the blue and green stations. We judge what kind of cyan we are experiencing based on how strongly we perceive the blue and the green stations in relation to each other. It is a qualified guess, based on an indirect means of detection.

IT IS NOT ALL CONES

On the surface of our retinas, in addition to the three types of cone cells, there is a fourth type of cell called a *rod cell*. Its function is to detect brightness and darkness. There are many more rod cells (about 90 million per eye) than cone cells, thus the black-and-white resolution of our eyes is much higher than the color resolution. Rod cells are very sensitive to light and will respond to as little as a single photon. Cone cells will not respond at that low intensity level, and this is why our ability to distinguish color decreases as light intensity fades.

Interestingly, the rod cells have a peak response to a particular set of color wavelengths that corresponds to a lime-greenish hue. Although rod cells don't seem to play a role in determining color, they are more responsive to light in this blue-green range than other frequencies or colors of light. This concept will be revisited in Chapter 10, on color dominance.

EACH OF US IS UNIQUE

I've qualified my statements about color by using phrases like "our vision system" and "human" evolution. This is because there are many types of vision systems in the animal world. Some insects have as many as 16 types of color-detecting cells in their eyes. House cats (and some humans who have one of several variations of color blindness) only perceive two primary colors because their eyes have only two types of cone cells (they are called *dichromats*). Some women have a fourth type of cone cell that has a peak response somewhere between the L and M cones, allowing them to see many more amber and yellow variations (*tetrachromacy*). For them, yellow is a fourth primary color.

For the rest of us, though, red, green, and blue are our additive primary colors. One thing that is surprising, though, even among all of us with three types of cone cells in our eyes, is that the distribution ratio of those cones varies widely from person to person, giving each of us a truly unique experience of color.

Among the 4.5 million cones in each of our eyes, one person might have values of 75% L cells and 20% M and another person might have 51% L with 44% M. S Cells seem to be more constant, with a 5% distribution around the retina. In addition to the ratios changing from individual to individual, each individual's pattern of cell arrangement is also unique. Perhaps this is one reason it is difficult to talk with precision about color. Each of our experiences of color is truly unique.

CONCLUSION

What we call primary colors—red, green, and blue—cannot be derived by mixing other colors of light together. They are a result of the structure of our eyes and correspond to the wavelengths to which our cone cells have their peak response. We perceive all of the other colors on the spectrum based on the relative detection response of our three types of cone cells. This is what makes additive mixing possible.

> *Tip:* *When choosing primary color filters for tungsten cyclorama equipment, it can be frustrating because the red tends to be so much more prominent than the blue and the green. Tungsten stage light contains much more red than the other two primary colors, and therefore primary colored filters will not deliver equal amounts of red, blue, and green light when filtering a tungsten source. Next time you design a cyclorama into a project using primary colors, try choosing a red gel that is more saturated (deeper) and blue and green gels that are less saturated (paler) and experiment with creating mixes around the new colors.*

PRACTICAL: EXPLORING THE SPECTRUM

Illus. 3.2.

In your light lab, obtain and set up a prism and a light source to re-create Sir Isaac Newton's experiment. Our three types of rod cells can easily distinguish red, blue, and green. But because of the relatively close wavelengths between blue and green, it is harder to judge the nature of colors between those two points. However, the spectral space (or distance between the relative wavelengths) between green and red is pretty large, so it is relatively easy to distinguish yellow from orange. Thus, the apparent banding of the spectrum is simply a technique of our vision systems to cope with the complexity of the spectrum. How many colors in the resulting spectrum can you name?

If you have access to any non-tungsten spotlight sources, look at them through the prism. How is the refraction different from the tungsten one? Set up a practical version of the visible spectrum with stage lights and gel color using the actual refraction as your guide. How many lights do you need to set up a reasonably blended facsimile of the refracted spectrum?

4.

OTHER SPECTRAL COLORS

CYAN AND YELLOW: POINTS ALONG THE VISIBLE SPECTRUM

When thinking about color, red, green, and blue are a great start. However, there is more to the spectrum than the three primary colors. As we saw in Chapter 3 (Primary Colors in Light), Newton posited that the spectrum had seven colors: red, orange, yellow, green, blue, indigo, and violet. But we now know that the spectrum is made up of a continuous band of frequencies. Newton and others, not knowing about frequency bandwidth, arranged the observed colors into a sectioned circle, like pieces of a pie.

If red, green, and blue are the primary colors, is there a hierarchy to the other colors on Newton's wheel? In Chapter 3, we talked about combining the primary colors in various amounts to arrive at the other spectral colors. For instance, if you mix equal parts of green and blue light from the same angle onto a surface, the result is cyan, a color that Newton did not distinguish. We call cyan a *secondary color*.

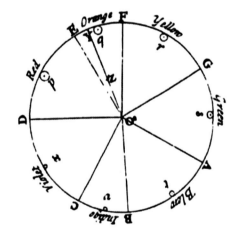

Illus. 4.1. Sir Isaac Newton's illustration of the observed spectral colors in English arranged in a circle.

Illus. 4.2. Mixing primary blue and primary green light creates a secondary color: cyan light. A video of this mix may be streamed here: http://silmanjamespress.com /colorandlight/videos/. (Move the slider bar to see this mix occur. At what point do you perceive the color as not being blue anymore? Are there other nameable colors along the path from blue to cyan?) Video by Edouard Getaz.

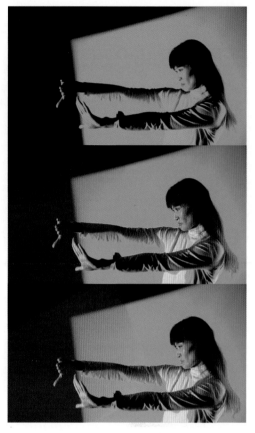

Illus. 4.3. Mixing primary green and primary red light creates a secondary color: amber light. A video of this mix may be streamed here: http://silmanjamespress.com /colorandlight/videos/. (Move the slider bar to see this mix occur.) Video by Edouard Getaz.

The additive mix of red and green lights yields yellow, sometimes called amber. Of course, for anyone who has come to working with light after learning how to subtractively mix colors in paint or dye this may seem counterintuitive.

Just as there are three primary colors in light, there are also three secondary colors, two of which are cyan and yellow. I haven't

Illus. 4.4. Mixing primary red and primary blue light creates a secondary color: magenta light. A video of this mix may be streamed here: http://silmanjamespress.com/colorandlight /videos/. (Move the slider bar to see this mix occur.) Video by Edouard Getaz.

Illus. 4.5. Three primary color sources mix to create secondary colors and a version of white light. Video by Edouard Getaz.

mentioned the third secondary color, and that is because it is a special color. When you mix red and blue light, the result is magenta, our third secondary color.

Magenta is a secondary color that can be formed by additively mixing blue (on the low end of the spectrum) and red (from the high end of the spectrum).

MAGENTA: A SPECIAL CASE

Let's go back to our spectrum chart:

Illus. 4.6.

Here, we can easily see how yellow fits in between green and red, but how does magenta fit in between blue and red, which are at opposite sides of the spectrum?

The answer is that magenta, a color that is somewhat like other spectral colors in terms of its saturation, doesn't exist on the visible spectrum. Magenta is a color that our brains create when our red and blue detection cones are stimulated at similar levels of intensity.

Illus. 4.7. The sensation of magenta occurs in our brains when we see light from both the infrared and ultraviolet ends of the spectrum.

When our eye receives light that has wavelengths that are at both the low end of visible light (near ultraviolet) and the high end of visible light (near infrared), it creates the sensation of the color magenta. Of the six primary and secondary colors that we have mentioned so far, magenta is the only one that does not exist within the spectrum (i.e., rainbows) and can only be made by mixing two other colors of light. Again, because of the way we detect color, most colors only exist as a mix between two or more primary colors, so experiencing magenta is no problem. But there is no single wavelength of light that corresponds to magenta.

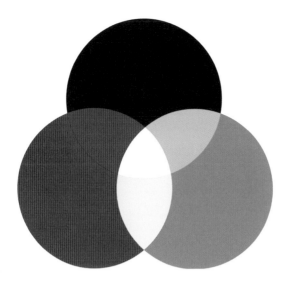

Illus. 4.8. A diagram showing the three primary colors of light, additively mixing to secondary colors and white.

TERTIARY COLORS

By mixing adjacent primary and secondary colors, we can create what are called *tertiary* colors. Violet, rose, and chartreuse are tertiary colors. In addition to these, Newton mentions yellow and he also includes orange in his list. Orange is like yellow in that it can be a mix of red and green light but with more red than green. We call orange a tertiary color, the third level in our hierarchy of colors.

Note that we're only nine colors into the description of colors and the definitions are already beginning to break down. Everyone may have an intuitive sense of the meaning of the color red. Would everyone have an understanding that "rose" is a mix of primary red and secondary magenta? Tertiary colors beyond orange, violet, and a few others are less commonly recognized. That is not to say that they are not useful or important, just that their naming is not understood universally across a randomized population of English speakers.

What is important to understand is that all of these colors—primary, secondary, and tertiary (with the exception of the special case of magenta)—are spectral colors. They each exist within their own small range of wavelengths along the visible spectrum. We perceive nonprimary colors as being derived from the primary colors, but this is the result of our vision system. All of the rainbow (spectral) colors correspond to actual single wavelengths of electromagnetic energy traveling through space. We see all of these colors because of some proportional response of our vision, but in their ideal state they are measurable single frequencies.

MIXING NON-ADJACENT WAVELENGTHS

There are, of course, colors beyond those that correspond to specific, single wavelengths of light. Lavender, khaki, and slate, for instance, are examples of colors that are not found in a rainbow. These colors are mixes of nonadjacent colors. Lavender, for instance, can be a mix of red and blue with some green light in it. This will be discussed further in Chapter 5 (The Color Circle and Color Spaces). For now, it is important to understand that there

Illus. 4.9. Non-spectral colors lavender, khaki, and slate.

are more colors in the world than exist along the spectral line. The spectrum is just a start to a whole world of colors that we can see.

CONCLUSION

Natural visible light forms a continuous and unbroken range of colors. We define three specific points along this spectrum as primary colors of light because we have found that we can combine these colors to arrive at other colors along the spectrum. There is a hierarchy to these colors that is based on how the primaries are mixed together. Roughly equal mixes of any two primary colors yield colors that we call secondary colors. A secondary color mixed with an adjacent primary color yields a tertiary color, of which orange is the best known. Other tertiary colors have names that are not commonly defined across the entire population; some examples are azure, chartreuse, and rose.

It is important to remember that our notions of color are subjectively human. The hierarchies of colors that arise from the primary, secondary, and tertiary naming conventions are the result of our evolutionary and cultural histories, not the actual nature of photons zinging around space.

Tip: Don't be restricted to primary colors when choosing colors for a cyclorama or other three-color additive system. Every color is capable of mixing with other colors, sometimes with surprising and beautiful results. Free yourself to experiment when choosing colors for a cyclorama or other intended additive mixing systems to make the most specific (and therefore interesting) choice for a scene or a show.

PRACTICAL: EXPANDING YOUR COLOR RESEARCH COLLECTION

Add onto your research collection with new categories of lighting interest. Collect images from print sources that connect feelings and situations to specific color palettes. Whenever you see an image that you like, add it to this collection so that it will become a part of your working research files. Now think of categories of images that correspond to emotional states or action words where color is used in an emblematic way. The important thing is that the collection of images is connected to things you find interesting or beautiful or somehow useful in the context of light and color storytelling.

5.

THE COLOR CIRCLE AND COLOR SPACES

A SCHEMATIC LOOK AT COLOR MIXING

Sir Isaac Newton created the concept of a *color circle*, where each color has an affinity with the colors next to it, but he left off magenta, the nonspectral secondary color. A color circle is a great way to visualize the proper placement for magenta and other nonspectral colors. Further scientific experiments have taught us a lot since Newton did his work with prisms, so we generally have slightly different colors listed in our modern-day color wheel.

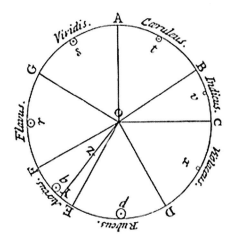

Illus. 5.1. Newton's color circle in Latin.

Imagine the spectrum printed onto a ribbon of paper.

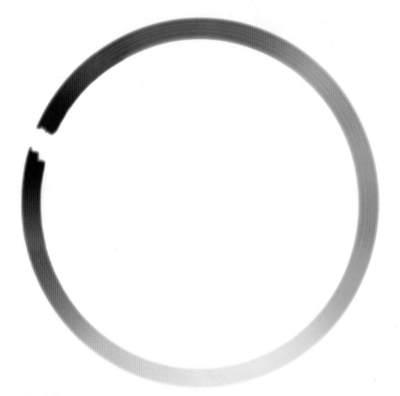

Illus. 5.2.

Now, in your mind, pick up the paper by the two ends and join them to form a circle with the paper ribbon on its edge. Here's something like what you would see:

Illus. 5.3.

A color circle is a schematic chart that shows the order of spectral colors. We place magenta where the two ends join, since it is the perceived result of mixing very low frequency visible wavelengths and very high frequency visible wavelengths of light. In our color circle, it is convenient to place the three primary colors (blue and green and red) equally spaced around the edge.

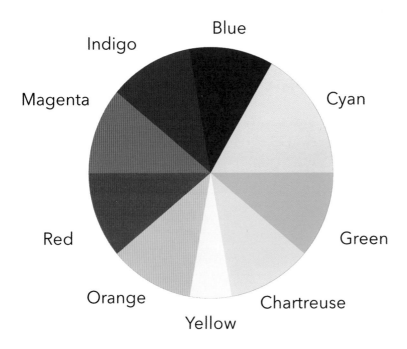

Illus. 5.4.

I always put blue at the top, for reasons that will become clear later. Next, at around 4 o'clock on the circle, I place green, and then finally I add red, at 8 o'clock. In between these places, at 2 o'clock, 6 o'clock, and 10 o'clock, I place cyan, yellow, and magenta, respectively. I usually draw my color circle with a gap where magenta is, to remind myself that it is a nonspectral color.

A NEW COLOR CIRCLE

We've talked about mixing two primaries together to get the secondary colors. It is also of course possible to mix three colors together. When we mix all three primaries together—red, green, and blue—in roughly equal proportions, we get a version of white light. You can see this every day on your computer monitor, which is made up of thousands of tiny pixels of red, green, and blue hues. By varying the amount of each color, the screen can display thousands, or millions, of colors.

Illus. 5.5. Here, three lights are mixing to create a version of white light. The component sources are revealed in the shadows created by the paper. Photo by Edouard Getaz.

You can also see this for yourself when working with light against a white wall. It has been common to filter three separate systems with the three primary colors to create lighting for a cyclorama. By varying the dimmer intensities of these three systems, one could create the secondary colors and also, though it is not often very satisfactory, a version of white with many variations.

Illus. 5.6.

Here's a new version of our color circle that approximates what happens when spectral colors are mixed together in various degrees. Notice that as the color moves in from the edge of the circle, representing the pure spectral colors, the colors get paler. We say that the colors are "desaturated" as they move toward the center of the circle.

The color circle concept has been developed over a 300-year period as a tool for artists and designers because it is a very convenient and easily remembered way to think about color. Notice how the primary and secondary colors are arranged: A secondary color is always directly opposite a primary color. These opposite pairs are called *complementary* colors and they serve some very useful purposes, as we will see. Like mixing the three primaries together, mixing a primary color with its secondary complement will produce a version of white light. Why is this? Let's look at some examples.

MIXING COMPLEMENTS

Red is a primary color, and its complement is cyan. When we mix the two additively, i.e., both coming from the same angle toward a common object, we see a version of white light. This is because cyan is already a combination of blue and green, the other two primary colors. So, when we mix a color with its complement, all three primary colors are present, and we will be able to achieve a version of white light.

Now let's go back to the drawing of the color wheel. Draw an imaginary line between red and cyan. See how it passes through

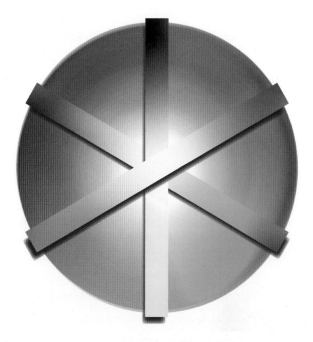

Illus. 5.7. Color wheel with three often used complementary pairs.

the white area near the center of the circle? Perhaps the color circle could be a graphing tool to predict the result of mixing any two complementary colors.

USING THE COLOR CIRCLE AS A PREDICTIVE TOOL

I want to be able to draw a line between colors to see what happens when they are mixed (additively), and I want the graph (the color circle) to accurately predict what will happen by mixing two complementary colors together. The color circle works as a general tool, but it has limits.

For example, remember that yellow is a spectral color; it exists in rainbows and in refracted sunlight. If I draw a straight line between green and red on the color circle, I arrive at yellow, but it is inside the circle. Yellow is a spectral color, so it should be on the edge of the spectrum, not within the circle. So, to better model what is happening, let's flatten out the secondary sides of the shape to form a triangle.

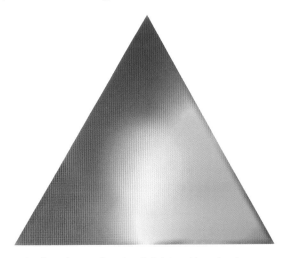

Illus. 5.8. Imagine flattening out the color circle into a triangular shape.

A COLOR TRIANGLE

In the color triangle, we still have all the elements from the color circle, but now the primary colors form the points of the triangle. The secondary colors are halfway along each line. Now perhaps it is easier to visualize what happens when we are mixing color. Any combination of red and green alone will always fall somewhere on the bottom edge of the triangle.

Illus. 5.9. A representation of the colors that will result from variably mixing red and green light.

This seems more correct, because we have already learned that all of the various shades between red and green are spectral colors. However, as soon as we add a little blue to the mix, it's easy to see how the resulting color would be pushed off the spectral line toward the center of the triangle. It can be very helpful to do this kind of graphing, not just with the secondary colors. The graphic depiction of visible color is called a *color space*.

The color wheel that we've been using, and the color triangle that we've just begun to look at, are the beginnings of arriving at an accurate representation of the colors that we see as a measurable color space.

Johann Wolfgang von Goethe (1749–1832), lawyer, writer, and artist, published a book called Theory of Colors *in 1810. Though he was largely incorrect in his hypotheses about the nature of color, his book was the first modern volume to attempt to deal with the nature of color perception (as opposed to Newton's focus on color's physical nature). Goethe also had the insight to arrange his colors into a triangle, though he was dealing with subtractive mixing instead of additive mixing. His book influenced many artists and philosophers in the following century and remains an important work in the history of Western art and thought.*

Illus. 5.10. Complementary colors can help give a composition visual interest.

TOWARD A MORE ACCURATE REPRESENTATION OF THE VISIBLE COLOR SPACE

At the beginning of the 20th century, a committee of scientists was formed to find the best shape for an accurate color space graph of visible light. Their work followed many attempts in the 18th and 19th centuries to accurately chart color space.

Professor Albert H. Munsell from the Massachusetts Normal Art School (now Massachusetts College of Art and Design, or MassArt) created a system of classifying colors based on their perceived perceptual differences in uniform steps. His system was the first to put colors in a three-dimensional space based on hue, value, and chroma, and while dealing with pigment color, his work is foundational to subsequent color spaces.

Let us recall our color triangle. If we rotate the points of the primary colors so that blue is on the bottom and green is at the upper left, we arrive at something that is close to the result of the committee's work.

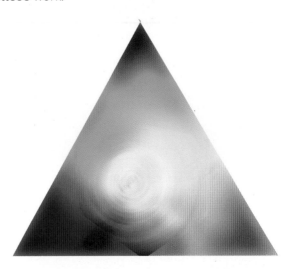

Illus. 5.11. The color triangle rotated to put blue at the bottom left corner and green at the top.

The 1931 Commission Internationale de l'Éclairage (aka CIE) color space chart is a more accurate version of the triangle that we just saw. In the CIE chart, just like in the color wheel and in the color triangle, the spectrum runs along the edge. The CIE chart does not attempt to join the two sides of the spectrum, however. Magenta

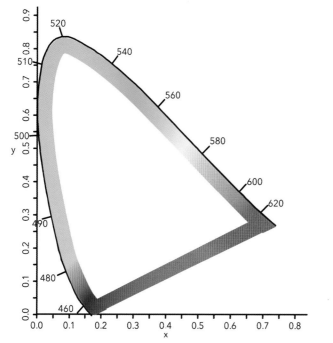

Illus. 5.12. The color triangle morphed into the more nuanced shape of the 1931 CIE xy(Y) color space. Illustration based on materials published by Commission Internationale de l'Éclairage.

exists along a straight line connecting the lowest frequency wavelengths with the highest frequency wavelengths, not unlike the side of our color triangle.

The big advantage of this shape over the color circle is that quantifiable colors, like paints and other pigments, can be definitively plotted, and we can begin to see relationships between them. However, there are still limitations to this graph.

The goal of all of color spaces is to accurately model our experience into a chart or graph that can be measured and manipulated both experientially and mathematically.

One big problem with this graph, though, is that the spatial distance does not always accurately reflect the perceptual difference between colors across the graph.

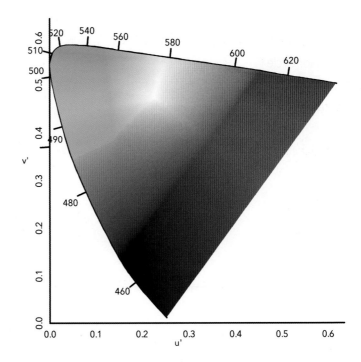

Illus. 5.13. A more accurate depiction of the colors of visible light: the 1976 CIE u'v' color space. Illustration based on materials published by Commission Internationale de l'Éclairage.

This color diagram, called *u'v'*, published in 1976, is a revision of one that was first published in 1931 (though it is still a representation of pigment colors and not color in light). In this more current graph, one can more accurately measure differences between colors as well as plot the effects of additive mixing between two or more colors.

I think that for artists and designers, it is good to be able to hold all these representations of color in our heads at the same time. The color wheel remains useful for remembering complements and primary and secondary colors. The CIE color spaces are useful for seeing a more complete representation of the colors that we can see. We'll revisit these charts throughout the book to see some other uses for lighting designers.

All of the color diagrams depicted thus far in the book, from Newton's color circle through the u'v' diagram, are two-dimensional representations. Notice that in all of these charts, there is no representation for black! To find black, we have to look at a third dimension of color and light, *luminance* (which for our purposes can be thought of now as a measure of relative intensity).

WHERE ARE BROWN AND GRAY AND BLACK IN THESE COLOR SPACES?

Illus. 5.14. These kinds of colors are not directly represented in most color charts.

I stated earlier that the CIE color space diagrams are graphs of all possible visible colors. This is true only as regards a certain level of luminance. Let's imagine for simplicity, if not complete accuracy, that the CIE color chart represents colors that are contained in a full spectrum source of light when it is at maximum intensity on a dimmer.

Now imagine what happens if you dim the output of that source. The colors will shift. Colors like brown and gray clearly exist in the world of pigment; for instance, wood is brown, stone is gray. When dealing with light, though, we see that these colors are reduced-output versions of colors that exist on the CIE chart. Brown is amber light as it appears to us at a lower level of output. Gray is white light at a lower level of output. A true gray color filter (neutral density) is like a window screen over a light. Some of the light is completely blocked, some of it goes through completely unimpeded, so that the color of the light is not affected. The filter only affects the amount of light that is getting through.

This kind of filtering does not in itself alter the color of the light. It only reduces the amount of light.

A "chocolate" or similar type of filter combines the effect of an amber filter (which removes a portion of the non-amber-producing colors—i.e., blues—from the light) and a gray, neutral-density-type filter in one convenient piece of plastic. The CIE color space graphs that we have seen are two-dimensional sections, or slices, of the full three-dimensional color space. In other words, these charts assume the full output of a given source.

WHY WOULD YOU WANT TO USE A NEUTRAL DENSITY FILTER? WHY NOT JUST DIM THE LIGHT?

Neutral density and other combination filters, like chocolate, exist to reduce the output of a luminaire without incurring the redshifting effect that happens when one diminishes an incandescent source with a dimmer. The color that the incandescent or tungsten source outputs is dependent on the voltage that is being applied to the lamp. A dimmer works by reducing the voltage, thus having the effect of cooling the filament that is glowing. As this happens, the spectral output of the lamp shifts toward red. Regardless of the filter that is applied to the light, the resulting color will shift toward red as the source is dimmed. Neutral density filters exist to reduce the output of a lamp without having to account for this redshift. This is especially important in film and video applications where the cameras or film stock have been aligned (keyed) to match a specific color of light so that one can achieve a clean white light on screen. The redshift effect shows up more dramatically in captured media—i.e., film and video—than it would on stage in a live performance. Redshift is a result of the technology of filament-based lamps and dimmers. Other sources that diminish, by either mechanical or other means, do not redshift as they dim. (I write about this more later on, especially in the chapters on LED lighting.)

CONCLUSION

There are many ways to illustrate the effect of mixing two or more spectral colors together. The classic color circle is not merely a convenient and useful tool for remembering the order of the colors in the spectrum, but also an easy way to schematically represent primary, secondary, and tertiary colors and their complements.

The CIE chart is an attempt at representing these same spectral and mixed colors in a graph form that provides some mathematical and visual advantages. In the CIE chart, colors can be plotted and the relative distance between them can be measured. In addition, once a group of colors are accurately plotted, it is possible to connect the points and discover the range of colors that occur by additive mixing between them.

Tip: An extremely useful primary/secondary complementary pair for the theater is blue and yellow. This combination comes up again and again in the repertory lighting plots of many ballet and opera companies. Explore how you can use variations of blue and yellow as additive pairs to create useful ranges of colors.

Illus. 5.15. In stage lighting, the blue-to-yellow complementary pair is very useful.

PRACTICAL: EXPLORING COLOR SPACE

As we have learned, there have been many attempts to describe the colors that we see in a comprehensive and objective way. This quest is important to us as lighting designers and artists because we increasingly use computers and other machines to help us create colors for lighting. If you want a four-color-mixing (red, green, blue, and amber) LED fixture to fade slowly from magenta to cyan, how is this fade accomplished? There are several possible answers, the most obvious is to just fade out the red emitter and fade up the green emitter. This is possible because magenta is composed of red and blue light, and cyan is composed of green and blue light. On the color wheel, such a fade path would look like this:

Illus. 5.16. The fade path from magenta to cyan that is most easily arrived at when using a four-color LED fixture.

In this case, the path follows the perimeter of the circle, not a straight line through the circle, and until recently this was the path that almost all control consoles would take.

The color fade between these two colors will look something like this:

Illus. 5.17. Here is the same color path straightened out along a line.

But if we wanted the fade from magenta to cyan to follow a different path, perhaps through white, how could we accomplish it?

Illus. 5.18. A color path with the same beginning and ending points that travels through white.

As we have learned, a color is desaturated (pulling it toward white) by adding its complement. In this case, to pull the color away from blue during the fade, we could add a little amber as the red is fading out, and then remove the amber as the green fades in. How much amber would be correct?

Here is where the circle model starts to fall apart. Because the color circle is not a mathematically accurate description of the relationships of the colors that we see, when we need the help of a computer to calculate the recipe of a color, or the path between two colors, we will need a better model. This is why the CIE color spaces are important to us, increasingly so as the color capabilities of our lighting fixtures become more and more sophisticated.

EXERCISE

In a light lab, arrange four separate fixtures and focus them to the same place on the white cyclorama. Color the fixtures (or program them to equivalent colors) with:

Primary Red (Roscolux 27)
Primary Green (Roscolux 90)
Primary Blue (Roscolux 80)
Secondary Amber (Roscolux 20)

then

1. Write a cue that creates a magenta color (blue and red).
2. Write a second cue that creates a cyan color (blue and green) that is programmed to fade over 20 seconds.
3. Watch the transition between the cues.
4. Try to figure out a way to transition through white instead of primary blue. How can you accomplish this with the fixtures that you have?

6.

ADDITIVE COLOR MIXING REVISITED

In a performance context, secondary colors can be very useful. Imagine three tungsten-based lights placed very close together. Each light is filtered to one of the secondary colors. The lights are focused to the same place on a surface.

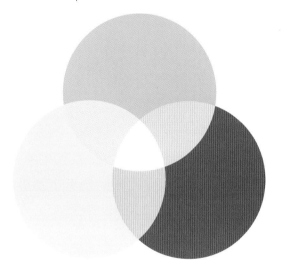

Illus. 6.1. Additive mix of secondary colors.

Remember the component parts of each of the secondary colors:

> **cyan** = blue + green
> **magenta** = blue + red
> **yellow** = red + green

When we mix cyan and magenta, we are actually mixing colors that our brains perceive with detectors that respond to wavelengths that correspond to primary colors. It's not that cyan isn't a spectral color, it's that the brain perceives that color only because both the blue cone and the green cone in the eye are stimulated.

In our brains, cyan is the result of a calculation. Our perception of cyan happens in our brain when cells that are tuned to green and blue both get stimulated. Therefore, when we mix cyan and magenta, our eyes see a color that stimulates all three types of cone cells.

Illus. 6.2. Additively mixing magenta and cyan. A video of this mix may be streamed here: http://silmanjamespress .com/colorandlight/videos/. Video by Edouard Getaz.

Illus. 6.3. Cyan and amber mixing together. A video of this mix may be streamed here: http://silmanjamespress.com /colorandlight/videos/. Video by Edouard Getaz.

COLOR & LIGHT

Since magenta is made up of blue and red, and cyan is made up of blue and green, the resulting mix (Illustration 6.2) is a color that has blue and green and red.

Illustration 6.3 shows cyan and amber mixing together.

It follows, then, that when we see a mix of any two secondary colors at similar intensities, all three primary color cones have been stimulated and we see a version of white. And here are magenta and amber:

Illus. 6.4. Additively mixing magenta and amber. A video of this mix may be streamed here: http://silmanjamespress .com/colorandlight/videos/. Video by Edouard Getaz.

Let's go back to our color circle and see it there.

Illus. 6.5. Secondary colors: cyan, magenta, and yellow on the wheel.

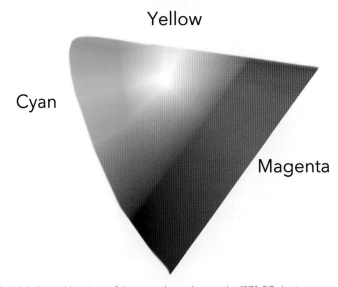

Illus. 6.6. General locations of the secondary colors on the 1976 CIE chart.

When you mix any two of the colors together, what you get is a version of white light. Perhaps it's a cool white (if mixing cyan and yellow) or a warm white (magenta and yellow), or perhaps it has a lavender quality (mixing cyan and magenta).

Here is where the CIE chart can be very useful. The shape of the CIE chart is an attempt to align the perceptual difference between colors with a mathematical distance that is consistent across the chart.

THE DISTANCE PROBLEM

Here's an example of a problem that was mentioned in the prior chapter with the color circle:

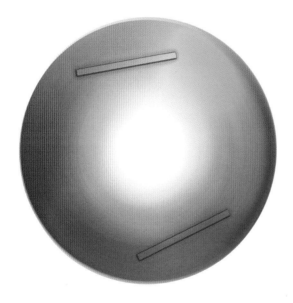

Illus. 6.7. Color wheel with two line segments of equal length.

Let's look at these two lines more closely. They are the same length, i.e., they cover the same distance within the circular color space. Now look at the colors at the end points of the two lines.

Illus. 6.8. Two equal-length line segments placed next to each other. The color differences between the ends of the lines are not equivalent even though the lengths are the same.

On the line at the top, both ends are versions of the color blue. On the line at the bottom, the right side is at green and the left is at a reddish orange. The bottom line covers three colors (orange, yellow, green) that are perceptually much further apart than the top line, which only goes from a redder blue to a greener blue. Choose any other two points within the color wheel where the distance between the points is the same as the above examples. An ideal color space would produce two colors of similar perceptual distance from each other any time the distance between the colors was the same. The color wheel clearly does not do this.

This is the big problem with the color wheel. The math involved in a) determining a color (as an example, by setting levels of LED emitters) and especially b) determining the difference between colors, does not align with most people's experience of the difference between the colors. This is what models and charts are supposed to do: accurately depict our experience of the real world in some measurable way. The CIE charts (and underlying formulae) are attempts to minimize this problem. Two equal-length line segments laid down anywhere within the CIE chart should fall on colors that can be said to have near equal perceptual differences to a viewer.

WHY IS THIS MATH IMPORTANT TO ME? I'M AN ARTIST!

As lighting designers, when we were using only tungsten lights and gels and our lighting computer consoles were designed only to manipulate dimmers, this problem didn't really concern us too much. However, with the advent of color-mixing luminaires, and especially LED-based lights, we now use computers to set, remember, and reproduce the color of the lights. And it is natural that we are now involved in a whole new level of color control and color movement over time. Control over how a light source transitions from one color to another and how it does so over a period of time has become extremely important to us. Manipulating this color path demonstrates a real need for plotting colors within an accurate color space. Chapter 5 (The Color Circle and Color Spaces) introduced the problem of moving from one color to another through a third color. Now, though, the lighting computer must be able to help us with this. If the computer can have an accurate way to model, i.e., plot and graph colors within a space that accurately represents our perception, it will be able to help make accurate and useful color paths.

PLOTTING AN ACCURATE PATH FROM ONE COLOR TO ANOTHER

While not perfect (created for pigments, not light, and based on a sampling of only a segment of the population), the CIE charts are a pretty good solution to accurately summarizing how we see color space. For the purposes of calculating colors that align with how we see, they are much better than a color wheel or color triangle. Nowadays, lighting designers are very involved with the problem of how to move from one color to another, as we can now plot not only the color of a luminaire on a computer console, but also the color path that the fixture will travel through during a fade from one color to another. The more control you want to have over the color output of your luminaires, the harder it is to deal with the inaccuracies of a circular color space.

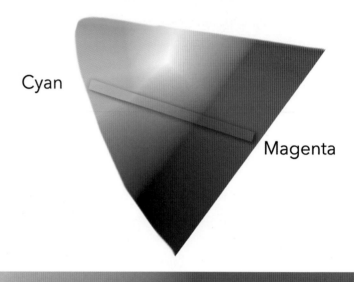

Cyan

Magenta

Illus. 6.9. A line plotted on the 1976 CIE chart between magenta and cyan.

This has been implied in the earlier discussions on color spaces, but here is another very important use of graphed color space. Because we can mathematically plot colors onto the CIE chart with some precision, we can also predict what will happen when those colors are additively mixed together. On the CIE chart, the result of additively mixing two colors is represented by a line that connects their two points. All of the colors that exist on that line can be arrived at by manipulating the relative intensities of the two colors.

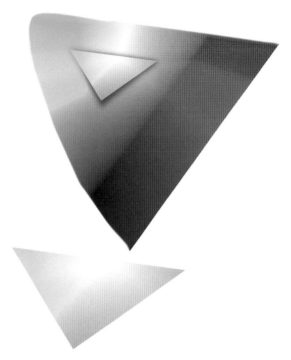

Illus. 6.10. Three colors plotted on the 1976 CIE chart. All of the colors within the triangle defined by these three points can be created by additively mixing the colors at the points of the triangle.

With three source colors, one can theoretically mix to all the colors within the resulting triangle.

Additive color mixing doesn't have to be across such a wide range as shown here. Imagine mixing two colors that are more closely related to arrive at a third color.

Illus. 6.11. Swatches for the colors at the points of the triangle.

VISUAL VIBRATO

I like to think of additive mixing from two or more different sources as a kind of visual vibrato.

Illus. 6.12.

"Vibrato: A slightly tremulous effect imparted to vocal or instrumental tone for added warmth and expressiveness by slight and rapid variations in pitch."

—Merriam-Webster's Dictionary

When a string player uses vibrato, the note that she is playing becomes, in a way, more perfect because it lives as a kind of idealized calculation in the listener's brain. It is a richer version of itself, embodying movement and an expressive feeling of being alive.

The same thing can be done with lighting by additively mixing two or more sources that arrive at the desired color through mixing. The color can become richer and more alive.

Depending on the physical distance between the two sources and the perceptual distance between the component colors, there will be glints of related shadow colors in places where only one of the lights can hit.

Additive mixing is a way of creating colors at the place where they touch a surface, not before. And when those surfaces are moving bodies, the colors can dance and play along with the movement of the performers. It can be thrilling.

WHEN TO USE ADDITIVE MIXING IN DIFFERENT SOURCES

Let's go back to the four reasons why we might use color.

1. *Can additive mixing create a realistic story point?*

Of course! Reproducing the light from a fire is a great example of a circumstance where additive mixing might serve a story. The light from a wood fire changes and morphs through colors from moment to moment. Combining several related flame-colored units into a system of firelight might be the best choice to evoke firelight. The color can then morph and dance in a way that evokes the flames of the fire. Another example in which additive mixing might help tell the realistic story is with patterned light. Imagine light filtering through a forest of trees. Would the light that reaches the path on the forest floor be only one color, or would it be a range of colors that are related to the many colors of leaves and flowers and other forest bits through which it traveled and was filtered? To express the richness of a particular forest, perhaps the patterned system of lights might be colored with a range of related colors.

2. *Can the use of additive mixing help communicate the intended style of the event to the audience?*

Absolutely, and perhaps here is its greatest use. By pushing the component colors away from the intended color target, you can increase a sense of theatricality. The stage can feel richer and more alive; in a similar way that a musical number can enhance and deepen our understanding of a character's emotions, using additive mixing can communicate, perhaps unconsciously, to an audience that this is the kind of place where people naturally break into song when the emotional energy requires it.

Illus. 6.13. The colors can be made richer and the shadows more interesting by using two colors to mix instead of just using the resulting mixed color as a single filter. Photograph by Edouard Getaz.

COLOR & LIGHT

The overall result is magenta light, but because red and blue sources are used to make the magenta, the overall space shatters into light of several related colors, creating a statement around the color.

This question of style is not limited to the musical theater. In the final scene of the realistic World War I drama *Journey's End*, the hero dies along with his bunker mates. The scene takes place at dawn. In my design, I used ellipsoidals on the floor from the sides that were colored in primary green and red. The units were placed very close together so that the component shadows were

Illus. 6.14. *Journey's End* at the Westport Playhouse. Directed by Greg Boyd. Scenery by Hugh Landwehr. Costumes by Linda Fisher. Lighting by Clifton Taylor. Pictured from left: Andrew Kirsch, Kieran Campion, James Black, and Mark Shanahan. Photograph by Victor W. Smith.

minimal, but they were there in the folds of the costumes and in the cracks of the scenery.

As the world around these men was literally cracking up and falling in, the lighting also was breaking up into its component parts. Probably no one who saw this play could have articulated this change in the lighting, but it was an essential component to the overall effect.

3. *Can additive mixing help light scenery or costumes?*

On a completely flat and smooth surface, using additive mixing to create a color is equivalent to finding the same color filter in a single source. Mixing, as on a cyclorama, is useful because it gives a designer a range of possible colors that can be changed from moment to moment.

Now, imagine a costume, perhaps a dress with lots of ruffles designed for a dancer. Would it serve the design intent of the costume to have multiple colored shadows in those ruffles? I can imagine both answers to this question depending on the piece, the costume, and the production.

4. *Can additive mixing serve us in helping to render space with more or less depth?*

On a cyclorama, absolutely, because by choosing to mix colors additively (and by separately channeling the lights across the length of the system), you can vary the color of the cyclorama along its length.

Look at this painting by J. M. W. Turner, *Fishermen at Sea*. See how the light in the sky is varied across the length of the painting, not just by intensity but also by color. In doing this, Turner

Illus. 6.15. *Fishermen at Sea*, by J. M. W. Turner. Courtesy of Tate Images.

enhances the sense of spatial depth in the painting, creating an enclosure of clouds and atmosphere that frames the subject of the little boat in the water. With enough control and additive mixing, you can vary the color across a system in similar ways.

Think of the component colors that you would use to additively create the feeling of Turner's sky with light on a cyclorama, and how, by varying intensities across the length of the cyclorama, you could create variations that evoke Turner's image. Of course, a painted backdrop and maybe some projections are also called for to complete the picture, but I'm thinking only of the lighting colors here to help make all this work.

The additive process is important both for creating a sense of depth and, given that a performance takes place over time, for allowing changes to occur in the lighting over a period of time. So rendering space has two components: spatial depth and time. Additive color mixing can assist in both tasks.

CONCLUSION

Additive mixing is an extremely important tool for designers in the theater and becoming ever more so. LED equipment takes this concept and builds component colors into a single fixture. Additive mixing yields all of the colors that such a fixture can produce. Whether there are three or seven colors in the LED fixture, to get the color that you want, you will mix different color emitters from within the fixture. But in addition to LEDs, consider the possibilities of mixing separate fixtures to arrive at a new color. You will find that charting the colors onto a CIE color space chart will help you to visualize the possible resulting color mixes, or perhaps the color circle is useful enough in helping you to make this visualization. Whatever tools you use, explore the possibilities of additive mixing in terms of storytelling, style, and enhancing the depth of your designs and the designs of your collaborators.

PRACTICAL: ADDITIVE MIXING AND SECONDARY COLORS

We have studied secondary colors in the preceding chapters, but I haven't really talked too much about why they are so useful to us in a performance context. The secondary colors are useful for several reasons:

- Any two secondary colors can be combined to create a version of white light. By placing two lamps next to each other with two different colors in them, but with the same focus, we can arrive at a whole range of colors beyond the two filtered colors. To get that range of colors from primary sources, we would need three lamps.

- Because of the way our eyes work, secondary colors appear to embody a range of color frequencies while remaining very saturated. At the same level of saturation, cyan can render more local pigment colors (in costumes and scenery) than blue or green. And the same goes for magenta and yellow.

When we mix secondary colors additively (again, additive mixing is when there are two sources from the same direction with two different colors), by varying the intensity of the two sources, we can arrive at a whole range of colors.

EXERCISE

In your light lab, arranged as in the schematic lighting plot shown in Illustration 6.16, design a series of lighting compositions and cues using only saturated secondary colors.

- Sunrise
- Morning
- Hot Afternoon
- Nighttime
- Campfire
- A Dance Hall

See how the secondary colors can be used alone and together to create a large range of lighting compositions. Always keep in mind creating a sense of a real source of light as well as visibility.

I'm not suggesting this as a solution for a real project. It's an exercise to practice looking at these colors and seeing how they could work in your compositions and to learn how versatile a limited system of colors can be when additively mixing them together.

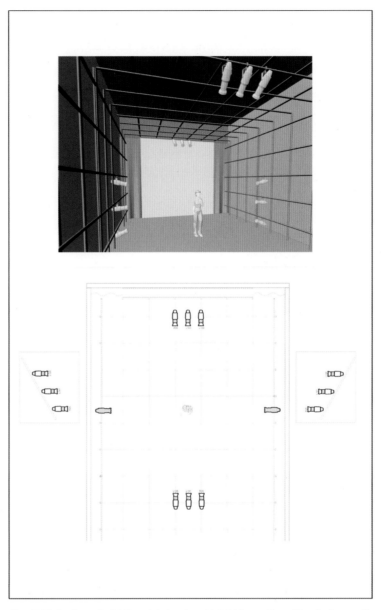

Illus. 6.16. A schematic lighting plot showing sidelight from either side of a figure with three lights each in Lee 126, Lee 141, and Roscolux 20. In addition, there should be three straight backlights and three straight front lights in the same colors. Each unit should have a separate control to create the exercise.

7.

SUBTRACTIVE MIXING

Illus. 7.1. The primary colors we learned in grammar school.

Subtractive mixing is very different from additive mixing. Subtractive mixing is the process of filtering a group of wavelengths out of a beam of white light. Whenever you use a color filter or program a color flag in a moving light, you are engaged in subtractive mixing.

In subtractive mixing, whether in light or in pigments like paints and dyes and ink, the secondary colors become the primary colors. Why is this? Think about how a color filter does its job. A magenta lighting filter works because it blocks the green wavelengths of light from a white source of light, letting only the blue and the red wavelengths through. In the film and video worlds, magenta filters are sometimes called "minus green." A cyan filter removes the red wavelengths from a white light source. Cyan filters could be called (but in practice are not) "minus red" filters.

If we combine this magenta filter with a cyan filter in the same light source, we will have filtered out all of the green (the magenta filter) and all of the red (the cyan filter). The result of combining these two filters will be the color blue. This is why subtractive color-mixing systems—paint, inkjet printers, or color-mixing filter flags within a luminaire—use cyan, magenta, and yellow colors as their primaries.

Yes, in elementary school we were taught that the primary colors are red, yellow, and blue. This was somewhat misleading even when talking generally about pigment, unless the blue in question has green in it (to move it toward cyan) and the red in question has blue in it (to move it toward magenta). As we saw in Chapter 2 (What Is Color?), color naming conventions have been the subject of inquiries by linguists for many decades, but now

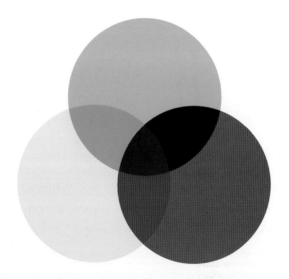

Illus. 7.2. Secondary colors in a subtractive (filtered) color arrangement.

is the time to let go of the idea that red, blue, and yellow are the primary colors for systems that use the base white of the paper or fabric to effect the resultant color. In a truly subtractive color situation, where a white background or white light is being filtered to create color, the three primary colors are cyan, magenta, and yellow.

You can use subtractive mixing in a non-mixing luminaire by combining two or more filters in a single light. I did just this in lighting a play on Broadway called *Frozen*. I needed to find a match where the tungsten lights would not clash with the arc-sourced moving lights in the show. The tungsten sources are much warmer than the cold, greenish Philips Discharge MSR575 source that we were using. I wasn't trying to match the output of the MSR source, which would have been technically impossible, but rather my goal was to find a color of light that worked with it in a compatible palette.

Illus. 7.3. *Frozen* by Bryony Lavery. Directed by Doug Hughes. Scenery by Hugh Landwehr. Costumes by Catherine Zuber. Lighting by Clifton Taylor. Pictured from left: Brian F. O'Byrne, Sam Kitchin, and Swoosie Kurtz. Photograph © Dixie Sheridan.

I found a color combination, Lee 201 + GAM515, that was able, at some intensity levels, to work together with the arc sources. The GAM color is called "plus green" because it very slightly filters out some of the magenta: both red and blue wavelengths. Lee 201 is a much stronger filter taking wavelengths of light in the warm (yellow, orange, red) end of the spectrum. By using these filters together in one color frame, I found a light that was slightly cooler and slightly greener than an unfiltered tungsten source and that could be balanced to work with the moving lights.

PRACTICAL: SUBTRACTIVE MIXING WITH MECHANICAL SYSTEMS

Prior to the advent of LED-based ellipsoidal units, manufacturers developed several mechanical-accessory solutions to achieving a computer-controlled color-mixing luminaire. The most commercially successful of these was the Wybron CXI, which used two strings of filters in a double scroller accessory that could fit into the filter slot of a standard fixed-focus luminaire. Other competitors were the Morpheus M-Fader and S-Fader brand scrollers, which employed three filter strings in a triple scroller accessory. Following those developments, a color-mixing system that is similar to the one found in most automated lights became available in a product called Sea-Changer that required the replacement of the center section of a standard ETC Source/4. Each of these products delivers a variable color-mixing solution for fixed-angle luminaires using the principals of subtractive mixing. Many lamp-based (arc and tungsten) moving lights offer color-mixing systems with subtractive color engines based on cyan, magenta, and yellow color "flags" that can variably mix colors.

EXERCISE

In your light lab, set up as many of these devices as you are able to assemble. As in the schematic lighting plot shown in Illustration 7.4, arrange the color-mixing luminaires all on one side of a mannequin. On the other side, set up a fixed-angle ellipsoidal with no attached device. Try to match the colors of actual gel filters with the devices from the other side. Many consoles come with libraries of gel colors. Look at the result of the computer-mixed color against a real filter from the other side. Can you make a better match?

Try the following filters to begin, and then choose four other filters that you like. Record the results on a form or spreadsheet as in Appendix B. I use a form like this whenever I create a color that I like or that will be useful to me in the future.

- No Color
- Lee 201
- Lee 161
- Roscolux 68
- Lee 119
- Roscolux 54
- Lee 142
- Roscolux 33
- Roscolux 27
- Lee 124

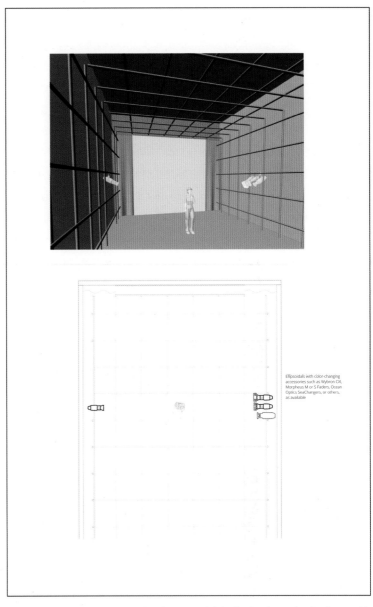

Ellipsoidals with color-changing
accessories such as Wybron CXL,
Morpheus M or 5 Faders, Ocean
Optics SeaChangers, or others,
as available

Illus. 7.4. A schematic lighting plot showing sidelight from either side of a figure with color-mixing devices on one side and a nonmixing ellipsoidal on the other. Each unit should have a separate control to create the exercise.

8.

WHAT IS WHITE LIGHT?

In the beginning of this book, I posed the question "Why color?" Why use color at all? That question seems to make sense because, in practical terms, we might think of color as something that is applied to white light via subtractive mixing. Color has a separate column in the spreadsheet paperwork that we use to specify a lighting plot, and color could be a filter that we put in front of a light, whether by cutting a piece of color media or programming a piece of glass to fall into the light beam within an automated fixture.

But now try to think of it in a different way, for we know that it is impossible to separate the idea of color from the idea of light. A photon at a specific level of energy reflecting off a surface will make that surface appear as a specific color. The perception of white light is caused by mixing enough of the visible colors together so that all three cell types are stimulated in some proportion. That seems to be a big definition, and in fact white light, under special circumstances, can be quite saturated. If we go back to our color circle, white light is at the center of the circle. But it's not just one point, but rather a surprisingly large range of colors that can be called white, depending on the full range of colors with which it is being seen.

KELVIN TEMPERATURE

In the 1920s and '30s, white light received a scientific definition correlating it to a heat temperature and an object (a black body emitter) that, when heated, emits visible light across the full spectrum of visible light. This is known as the Kelvin scale (designated by the symbol K) and it can be plotted within our existing color spaces. The temperature to which the object is heated corresponds to the Kelvin temperature of the color of the light.

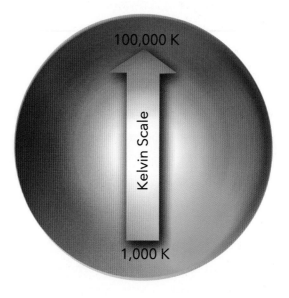

Illus. 8.1. Kelvin temperature scale plotted on the color circle.

Again, here it is in our color circle. As the Kelvin scale goes up, white light gets cooler, i.e., it approaches blue. Typical practical Kelvin temperatures range from 1500 K to 7000 K. Incandescent and tungsten lamps are typically measured at about 2600 K, sunlight is around 5500 K to 6500 K.

Here is the 1976 CIE color space chart, showing how Kelvin temperature is more accurately mapped from infrared up to cool whites.

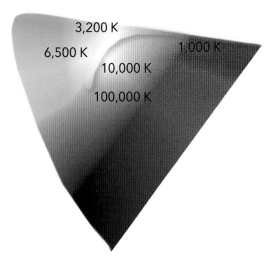

Illus. 8.2. Kelvin temperature scale loosely plotted onto the CIE 1976 u'v' color space diagram.

LIMITED SPECTRUM SOURCES AND WHITE LIGHT

Again, a black body emitter is an object that when heated emits light across the entire visible spectrum. The CIE color chart is based on this type of full spectrum source. However, there are sources of light such as HID or sodium vapor that do not output all of the spectral colors, and the CIE chart does not make plotting the color from these sources easy.

When I wrote about the problem of mixing tungsten sources with the MSR moving lights in Chapter 7 on subtractive mixing, I touched on this problem. It is practically impossible, and economically unfeasible, to filter a full spectrum source to match the spectral wavelength signature of a spiky arc source.

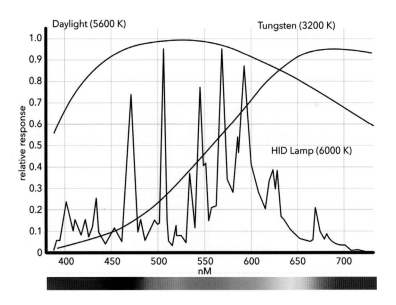

Illus. 8.3. A schematic diagram of the relative spectral components of tungsten, daylight, and HID sources. Data source: *About Lighting: Color Temperature of Metal Halide Sources* by Mike Wood (at https://www2.highend.com/support/training/colortemp.asp).

With arc fixtures, fluorescent fixtures, and LEDs, certain colors in the spectrum are simply not present in the output. No affordably available theatrical filters exist that could mask out specific wavelengths to make a tungsten fixture match the spectral signature of a fluorescent tube.

A non–full spectrum source can produce a version of white light and even have a measurable Kelvin temperature, but it will not be equivalent to a full spectrum source at the same Kelvin temperature. Nor will it look exactly the same in every side-by-side comparison, especially when it is reflected off differently colored costumes and scenery.

The term for talking about this is *color rendering*. Color rendering is a way of describing a given white light's ability to produce colors that a local object can reflect back. We say that a light can render a color when the component colors needed to accurately see a local color, like a pigment, are present in the spectral power distribution of the source light. This is a different concept than talking about a white light's color temperature. There is a measurement for this called Color Rendering Index, or CRI. This is an outdated measurement and it is being replaced as of this writing with a new standard called TM-30-15 (see the Glossary), which is also commonly known as just TM-30.

Because the source lamp in an arc source has a spiky spectral signature, the full color space that it produces will also always be spiky, no matter what filter is applied to the light. This means that every lamp source produces its own unique color space. Even with 4,000 color filters currently on the market, an arc-sourced luminaire can still produce colors that a tungsten-based luminaire cannot reproduce, and vice versa. This, of course, can be an asset or an impediment. Theatrical lighting designers often use multiple source types within a show. Non–full spectrum sources are covered more in Chapter 12 (Color Rendering, Limited Spectrum Sources, and New Color Spaces).

This matters because, if a light source cannot render a color properly, that color will not be seen properly, and the work of picking a paint color will have been for naught. TM-30 is a complex measurement system that, while outside the scope of this book, is well worth exploring.

WHITE BALANCE AND PROJECTION

When video projections are incorporated into designs, it is important for the lighting designer to consider the color integration of the overall visual design. This means harmonizing the chosen white of the lighting to the chosen white of the projections. Both the lighting designer and the projection designer share in this responsibility.

If the projection is using an arc source (like most LCD technology projectors), its white will have a higher Kelvin temperature than tungsten-lamped stage lights. This difference may be desirable but often does not make visual sense. Because the lighting designer is probably working with higher lumen output equipment, it is often more practically feasible for the lighting to balance to the projection rather than the projection balancing to the lighting. This is because, with lower output projectors, it is often not possible to lose any brightness out of the projector just to see the desired images. White-balancing a projector down to tungsten level Kelvin will almost always reduce its brightness. As projector technology continues to advance and projectors get brighter, this is becoming more of a collaborative decision about the white that fits the overall desired visual statement. This is a real advantage of LED-based luminaires because the lighting white point is a programmable choice for every moment.

All these discussions around white balance and white point lead us, though, to a larger issue, the subject of this chapter: What is white light? Or, more practically, what will a viewer of a visual composition accept as white light?

VARIABILITY OF THE PERCEPTION OF WHITE

Our perception of white light isn't limited to that thin line of colors described by the Kelvin line in the CIE color space. Depending on the entire composition, a huge range of colors near the center of the color space could be accepted as white, depending on the other colors in the visual-image color palette.

With some exceptions, our brains assign the least saturated color of almost any composition to be the white value. Illustration 8.4 shows two colored squares next to each other in three pairs. Try to look at only one pair of colors at a time and isolate your view to within the black frame.

For most of us, over a bit of time our eyes will push the least saturated color toward white. The brain assigns the least saturated color in a given composition to be white.

As pairs of colors develop sequentially, the more saturated color of one pair becomes the less saturated color in the next pair. The juxtaposition of a then-more-saturated color causes our brains to desaturate the lighter color and assign it as the new white point of the composition.

CONCLUSION

"White light" is a term with many meanings. Our brains construct the idea of white light based on the entire visual composition of the moment. In other words, our brains assign one of the colors in the composition as white in order to calibrate the rest of the composition. In a highly saturated visual composition, what is perceived as white can itself be relatively saturated. The lighting designer can decide what white will be in a given scene and build the rest of the color composition around that. Often I do just that when choosing colors. First I decide what the white will be, and then I build the other colors of the composition around that white.

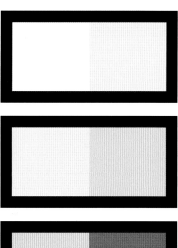

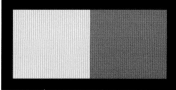

Illus. 8.4. In these three color bars, the color at the right of the upper bar is the same as the color at the left of the bar immediately below it. Would you have guessed that they are the same color? Our perception of a color is dependent on its surroundings; in other words, the full palette of colors in which that single color exists changes our perception of that color. Our perception of any given color is not fixed but dependent on the specific palette of colors in which it appears.

PRACTICAL: VARIABLE WHITE PERCEPTION IN LIGHT

(*Note: While this demonstration is useful as a part of a book to show a concept, it's actually magical to see it live, in stage light.*) In a light lab, set up a mannequin or a model and a pair of lights—head-high dance boom lights from either side of the model work best. It's also easiest to see this demo if the mannequin or helper model wears something white. Start with both sides in "no color," assuming you're using tungsten-based luminaires.

Now change the stage left side to a very pale pink. For this demonstration, I like GAM 107. Look at the model. Can you see the pink from the stage left side? Afterwards, keep the GAM 107 on the stage left side and change the stage right side to GAM 105. Look at the model again. See how the stage left side now appears to be the white side? Now, change the stage left side to GAM 130 and look again. What was the saturated side with GAM 105 will now appear to be the white point. You can continue this with Lee 328 and finally Roscolux 39.

As the colors are saturated, what was the more saturated color will become the reference white when placed against a color that is even more saturated. Why is this happening? Think for a moment about the purpose of vision: survival and hunting. Our eyes are assigned the task of gathering as much information as possible about the scene before us. Our visual system is evolved to look for contrast and increase it whenever possible.

We enhance the contrast of every scene that we look at in order to gain the most information from it. This happens subconsciously and automatically, but it leads to the variability of color perception depending on the entire composition. For example, there is no common or constant experience of a pale amber color filter. Our perception of that color is dependent on how it is used within a composition.

Note that the colors are contained within a black frame. This is vital because, if a pure white frame were exposed, it would be the white reference for your eyes. In the theater this is important too, because we must control the entire visual field for the audience so that what we are setting up as reality is a complete picture.

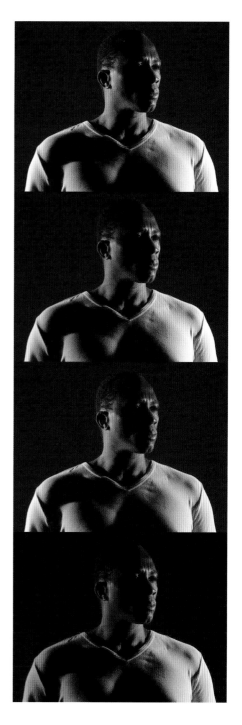

Illus. 8.5. This practical on a model shows increasing saturation in steps. In each successive photograph, the side that was previously perceived as colored pink light has not been changed. The perception of white is a value judgment that is composition dependent. Photographs by Edouard Getaz.

9.

SATURATION

Saturation is a property of color. A color becomes *more saturated* as it approaches the spectral color, or the outer edge of a color space. A perceived lighting color becomes *less saturated* as more wavelengths of complementary colors are mixed together. The color circle is a useful tool.

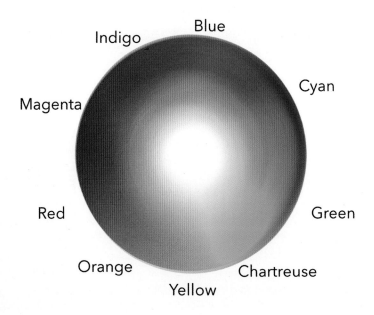

Illus. 9.1. The color circle with primary and secondary color names.

A REFRESHER ON COMPLEMENTS

An artistic definition of color complements is two colors that, when combined additively, desaturate each other and mix to a version of white. We saw this effect in Chapter 6 on additive mixing. On the color wheel it is very simple: Complementary colors are on opposite sides of the wheel. When looking at the CIE color space, it is perhaps not as intuitive, but it is a similar concept: A complementary pair of colors are those that are connected by a line passing through, or near, the chosen white point of the color space, on opposite sides of the shape.

As we have learned, the artistic definition of white light is broader than a technical definition of the white point. It is enough to remember that the complement of blue is yellow; the complement of red is cyan; the complement of green is magenta. Like so many things about color, complements are a mental construct of our brains and visual systems. There is no intrinsic property of color complements outside of our perception.

Complements are interesting to us as lighting artists because of their ability to desaturate each other. Start with a primary blue light on a subject. Additively mix in some yellow light (blue's complement) from another source from the same direction. Watch what happens. As the yellow increases in intensity, the blue becomes less saturated, and the resulting mixed color moves toward white.

Illus. 9.2. Complementary colors desaturate each other when mixed additively.

COLOR FATIGUE AND SATURATION

The word "performance" implies an art form that takes place over time. Time is an important factor in lighting design. Previously, I have talked about how the perception of color is variable and dependent upon the context of the palette of the entire visual composition, but the perception of a color is also malleable and dependent on the length of time the viewer is looking at the composition. Especially when viewed in isolation, a very saturated color will be desaturated by a viewer's brain over time, moving it toward the center of the color space, toward white. If you can move to a darkened viewing space, try this experiment. Stare at this blue color panel for 15 seconds, then move on to the explanatory text.

Illus. 9.3.

After a while, your brain gets tired of the blue and normalizes it. The perception of blueness becomes less and less intense over time. This effect is called *color fatigue*. Your brain adjusts its perception and recalibrates what it is seeing as a new version of white.

Because of this mental recalibration, when a new color is introduced it can be quite startling. Stare at a saturated color for a period of time and then quickly introduce white. Having calibrated itself to the original saturated color, your brain will push the new color toward the complement of the original color. Try it here. Look at the original color for 30 seconds in a darkened room, then see what happens when the image changes to white.

Illus. 9.4.   Illus. 9.5.

Did you see the cyan afterimage appear? This happens because the cones in your eyes that detect red got tired, reducing their ability to send data to the brain. When the square was changed to white, the tired red-detecting cones were a little slower in seeing the change in color and, as a result, you saw a version of white without red. Because of fatigue, your vision became biased toward cyan, red's complementary color. Over time, the red cones in your eye recover, the perception of cyan fades away, and the color is seen as white.

This effect happens with all saturated colors seen in isolation. The classic example in the theater is a red act curtain. Blues, greens, and cyans will appear much more vivid after the audience has had their retinas filled with a field of red before the performance.

Issues of color fatigue increase with color saturation and also over time. One solution to the problem of color fatigue is to provide the viewer's eyes with a complementary color somewhere in the composition that matches the level of saturation of the original fatigue-causing color. The complementary color does not have to match the volume of the original color. Often a relatively small amount of complementary color in a composition can solve the color fatigue problem.

> "During a rehearsal of Cave of the Heart *I had a wall of hot red light against the backdrop. The light was intensified until the curtain fell. I told the electrician to 'wash it out'—to cut the lights. He threw the switch and because the red lights were so violent, the eye was left with the impression of gray-green light bathing the stage. This lasted for only seconds—but it had the effect of turning the dancer's world suddenly to ashes."—Jean Rosenthal, from* The Magic of Light

FIND THE MISSING COLOR

If there is no complementary color in a given visual composition, the visual system will create one on its own. Here is a setup where a figure is lit in a series of pink colors from the side. A clear incandescent light fades up onto the front of the figure. See what happens with the clear front light as it fades up.

Note that the clear front light looks green on the figure. Why is this? Remember that the purpose of our visual system is to provide us with as much information about what we are looking at as possible. In order to increase the contrast, the brain will push its perception of colors away from each other in the color space. If the primary purposes of our visual system are to a) identify enemies, b) identify food, and c) identify mates (I don't purport to know the order of these three things!), then contrast and edge detection become super-important.

In the all-pink scene (a monochromatic visual composition), the white front light introduces wavelengths of pink's complement, green, into the composition. The viewer uses that green and pushes the white light toward green in order to find as much contrast as possible. This happens as soon as a composition becomes polychromatic. To correct for this, maintain the scene's monochromatic

Illus. 9.6. Here's an example of a monochromatic pink/magenta composition when clear tungsten light is added. The clear source shifts visibly to green. A video of this may be streamed here: http://silmanjamespress.com /colorandlight/videos/. Video by Edouard Getaz.

color scheme and keep the front light in the same monochromatic color group as the rest of the lights, i.e., remove the green from it and push it back toward pink. When evaluating a monochromatic palette, your visual system will only seek to push the contrast within that palette, as we saw in Chapter 8 on white light.

Here is another example of this polychromatic color shifting. This time the figure is lit with a palette of deep blue colors. See what happens as the same clear front light is slowly brought up.

Illus. 9.7. Here the front light is corrected by a slightly pink filter that allows the viewer's eye to perceive it as white light. A video of this may be streamed here: http://silmanjamespress.com/colorandlight/videos/. Video by Edouard Getaz.

Illus. 9.8. Adding a clear tungsten source to a monochromatic blue composition will shift the clear source toward yellow. A video of this may be streamed here: http://silmanjamespress.com/colorandlight/videos/. Video by Edouard Getaz.

COLOR & LIGHT

This time, the white front light was pushed to yellow, blue's complement. The same color front light will be pushed in two different directions depending on the surrounding palette. In one composition the white light turns green, in another it turns yellow. Color is malleable and dependent on the context of the palette in which it is seen.

Illus. 9.9. Here, this same composition has been corrected by the addition of a pale blue filter that once again allows the eye to perceive the clear source as white light. A video of this may be streamed here: http://silmanjamespress .com/colorandlight/videos/. Video by Edouard Getaz.

DEEP SATURATION AND THE ILLUSION OF DARKNESS

Think about these two statements:

- The opposite of light is darkness.
- The opposite of white light is saturated (spectral) light.

If we substitute "white light" for "light," is it possible that saturated light can stand in for darkness?

There are many times when we want a viewer to believe that there is darkness in a composition, but we don't want it to actually be dark. Color can help us to communicate the idea of darkness while allowing a performer to be seen.

Illus. 9.10. The intense blue from the right side becomes the shaded side for the viewer. It is a controlled shadow that reveals the spectacular dancer Terese Capucilli and makes a statement about the world that she inhabits. *Requiem* for the Buglisi Dance Theatre. Lighting: Clifton Taylor. Costume: Christina Gianinni. Photograph by Kristin Lødøen, 2007.

In the ballet *Requiem* for the Buglisi Dance Theatre, I used very saturated blue as a low sidelight. This gave the viewer the opportunity to both see the dancer's movements and to understand that it was in shadow. I used the saturated blue because it was recessive under the strongly sourced diagonal backlight. By using the very deep color from a low angle I was able to fill in the shadows of her figure and reveal the form of her back, while still making it clear that the key source of the light for the scene was from the backlight.

Tip: Deeply saturated colors can be thought of like a painter might think of a glaze. They can tone an entire composition, shifting it to a richer palette.

CONCLUSION

Saturation is a property of color. As any light moves from white toward the spectral edge of the visible color space, it becomes more and more saturated. We can mix very saturated complementary colors (additively, where both sources are coming from the same direction) to arrive at paler colors because complementary colors desaturate each other.

Over time, vision gets fatigued by large areas of saturated color and the viewer will naturally desaturate these color areas. One way that this can be counteracted is to provide contrasting colors within or around the visual composition, to allow the eye to calibrate the colors within the full scene.

Our visual systems have a preference for contrast and will seek it out and enhance it when possible. We do this with both dark and light contrast for monochromatic palettes, and color contrast for polychromatic palettes. This phenomenon is responsible for the apparent saturation of very pale compositions where very little real contrast is presented.

> **Tip:** When thinking about solving a problem that you might be having with a color, imagine the most saturated version of the same color. Would moving it one way or another along the spectrum help to solve the problem or make the composition better? Now, think about the level of saturation of the actual color, then ask yourself, would saturating or de-saturating this color help to solve the problem?

PRACTICAL: PALE TINTED COLOR PALETTES

In this chapter, we explored the idea of color saturation and the effect of very saturated colors on the brain. Now explore these concepts with less saturated colors.

1. Light a figure with pale lavender light from two opposite directions. If you are using color media, start with Lee 142. Over time, do you see the effects of color fatigue with this pale color? Does the color appear less and less saturated?
2. Add two more lights in tungsten no-color (3200 K) onto the figure from the same directions as the lavender lights, and construct a cue that switches instantly to the clear lights. What color do you perceive the new lights to be when the switch happens?
3. Now color the new lights with a pale green (lavender's complement). Try Roscolux 88. Slowly fade the green lights up and see how they move the lavender light toward white.

4. Now only light the figure with lavender with one of the two lights. Let your eyes adjust to this scene. Now slowly fade up the green light from the opposite side of the figure. Do the two lights now look more saturated?

5. Try these experiments again with even paler colors, perhaps Roscolux 53 and Roscolux 87. Can you still see these effects?

10.

COLOR DOMINANCE

Because we live on this planet with our sun and our specific atmosphere and because of our evolutionary history as a species, we do not perceive all colors equally. Though we can talk about red or yellow or blue as all being spectral colors and having a kind of equivalence, the fact is there are hierarchies of color perception in our brains. In these hierarchies, we assign an importance to yellow that exceeds that given to blue. In any pair of colors, our visual system automatically assigns one of the colors to be dominant and the other to be recessive. This concept is vitally important when working with color and light.

Josef Albers, the German-American artist and educator, studied this issue in rigorous detail. His book *Interaction of Color* is a highly recommended read for everyone interested in the subject of color in art and design.

TWO-DIMENSIONAL SPACE: SUBJECT AND FIELD STUDIES

Notice how the blue square in the center of this composition (Illus. 10.1) appears to recede while the outer squares seem to advance.

Illus. 10.1. See how the blue square in the center of this composition seems to recede? Just by reversing the colors, the composition can appear to recede or advance.

Below is a similar composition with yellow at the center. See how the center seems to advance toward you and the outer squares recede away from you? Now let's look at a similar demonstration using an onstage figure.

Illus. 10.2. Now the center, colored yellow, appears to advance.

Illus. 10.3. The figure in blue recedes into the yellow background. Photograph by Edouard Getaz.

Illus. 10.4. With the colors reversed, now the yellow figure advances from the blue background. Photograph by Edouard Getaz.

The same effect happens with lighting color. The same blue and yellow colors that we used in our additive mixing in Chapter 6 (Additive Color Mixing Revisited) are used in these photos. Earlier, I wrote about how complementary colors desaturate each other. Look at this example to see how color dominance plays a role in the desaturation process.

When you start with the blue figure and add yellow, the blue is desaturated until it becomes a version of white.

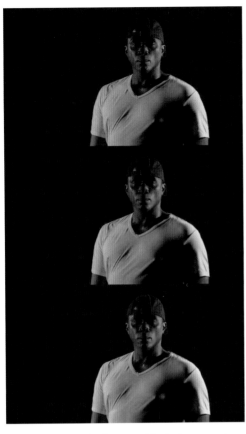

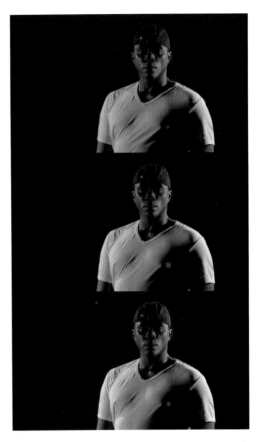

Illus. 10.5. Look at the figure's T-shirt. In the areas where the blue and yellow light are both present, watch how the yellow light increasingly desaturates the blue, making it less blue and more white. A video of this may be streamed here: http://silmanjamespress.com/colorandlight/videos/. Video by Edouard Getaz.

Illus. 10.6. As the yellow light increases in intensity it dominates the recessive blue light, overtaking it and turning the figure's T-shirt yellow. A video of this may be streamed here: http://silmanjamespress.com/colorandlight/videos/. Video by Edouard Getaz.

But what happens when you continue to increase the intensity of the yellow until their intensities are equal? Let's see.

This time, so much yellow gets added that it takes over the blue. What is happening here? Why is the yellow stronger than the blue at equal intensities? Both the blue and the amber are spectral colors, i.e., they exist on the spectrum. But our brains do not perceive them equally. This is an important concept to think about and understand. Not all colors are perceived equally. Our brain prioritizes colors in a composition and orders them according to that priority. In this arrangement, the yellow dominates the blue, and we say that the blue is recessive and the yellow is dominant.

There is no absolute hierarchy across the entire spectrum, because color is palette-dependent. A color that is dominant in one palette may be recessive in another. We can set up a situation where a particular yellow dominates a particular blue. But then introduce a pale green, and it is possible to make the yellow become recessive to that green.

Dominant and recessive color hierarchy happens in the viewer's brain. The phenomenon happens because of the particular evolution of our eyes and brains. Other animals with different visual systems have different hierarchies of dominant and recessive colors. It is a complex idea because it depends on the context of the color palette in a given visual field. It is made more complex because light works in three dimensions.

A SCIENTIFIC EXPLANATION

When dealing with spectral colors, only comparing single wavelengths of light, the CIE has worked out three functions that are related to the phenomenon of color hierarchy. These are called the *luminosity functions*. "Luminosity" is a word that refers to the relative brightness of something. The three functions are related to the amount of light in a given scene, one for full light situations (*photopic*), one for dark situations (*scotopic*), and one in between (*mesopic*). The graph shows a schematic representation of the full light and dark functions. The x-axis describes wavelengths of light, and the y-axis

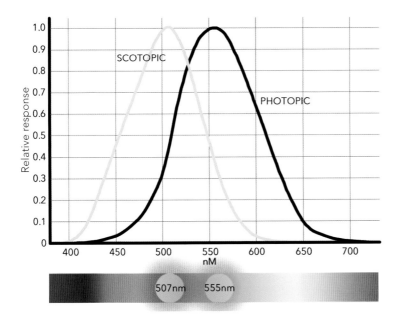

Illus. 10.7. Luminosity function graph showing the peak response to the light spectrum of rods and cones in our eyes. Illustration based on data republished in the Wikipedia article "Luminosity Function."

is a representation of human response to these spectral colors. The normal light graph peaks around yellow-green wavelengths. The low light graph peaks in the area around green-blue colors.

The luminosity functions are useful for understanding the subject of color dominance, but in practice we don't deal solely with spectral colors, which complicates the issue. Following are some guidelines for thinking about color dominance. Remember that these are general guidelines, and are therefore somewhat subjective.

- Secondary colors tend to dominate adjacent primary colors.
- Less saturated colors tend to dominate more saturated colors.
- When dealing with equal or near-equal levels of saturation and intensity, warm colors (ambers, oranges, and reds) tend to dominate cool colors (blues and greens).
- Lavenders are usually the most recessive colors in a palette.

- Magentas are often dominant colors in a palette.
- Pale yellow-greens are usually the most dominant colors in a palette.

THREE-DIMENSIONAL SPACE: COLOR EFFECTS WHEN LIGHTING A FIGURE

Illus. 10.8. As the yellow sidelight fades up and hits the front of the figure, it completely takes over the blue light. A video of this may be streamed here: http://silmanjamespress .com/colorandlight/videos/. Video by Edouard Getaz.

Just as the question "What is white?" can only be answered in the context of a color palette, questions of color dominance can only be answered within a particular composition. Almost everything about color perception is relative. When we additively mixed the blue and amber, we saw that the amber overtook the blue at high enough intensities. Let's look at a situation where the additive mixing happens, but where the two source lights are not next to each other. Here is our model lit with blue backlight.

As we add amber sidelight to the composition, see how it desaturates the blue. In places where both lights touch the figure, the amber becomes whiter. Even when the blue is at maximum intensity at the end of the clip, there are very few places where you can see the original blue color. It is visible only in the places where the yellow light is not touching because of its angle.

Here is the same setup with the colors reversed.

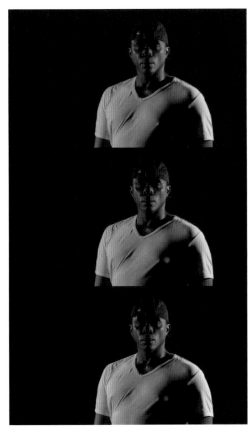

Illus. 10.9. Here, the same colors are used, but rearranged in the composition so that the yellow (dominant color) light is the backlight and the blue light is coming from the side. This arrangement allows for more places on the figure where only the blue light, which is recessive, appears and results in a more three-dimensionally rendered figure. A video of this may be streamed here: http://silmanjamespress.com /colorandlight/videos/. Video by Edouard Getaz.

Illus. 10.10. By simply rearranging the colors in your composition, you can completely change the perception of those colors as well as the audience's understanding of space, depth, and meaning. Photographs by Edouard Getaz.

In this arrangement, it is easier to see three distinct colors. The yellow backlight halos the entire figure. Where the two colors are mixing, there is a warm white, bringing the backlight forward around the figure. In addition, the blue is very apparent now, because there are places on the figure where the backlight doesn't touch and therefore cannot overwhelm the recessive blue color.

Just by rearranging the two colors, the composition changes completely. Because light works in three-dimensional space, the angle of light becomes an extremely important factor in a composition. By putting the dominant color in the back, it can help separate the figure from the background and allow places for the recessive color to be seen without being overwhelmed by the dominant color. The composition becomes more dimensional, with more contrast. We can say that it has more depth.

> *"Contrast = Interest"*
> *—Sal Tagliarino*

RECESSIVE COLORS AND SHADOWS

Think about shadows for a moment. A broad definition of a shadow might be "the absence of a light." This makes sense in a lighting composition where there is only one light. But think about shadows that occur on a bright day outdoors. They are created in places where the direct sunlight cannot hit. But the shaded area still has light illuminating it. Outside, on a sunny day, what are the other light sources besides the sun? The sky itself is a light source. All the sunlight being reflected off the particles in the atmosphere is itself a light source.

The sky is a special kind of light source, though, because it surrounds a figure with a relatively equal amount of light. On a bright day, the sky itself does not produce shadows because of its size. Rather, it fills in the shadows caused by other sources like direct sunlight. This is actually quite difficult to achieve on stage. Unlike the sky, theater spotlights are essentially point sources. Like sunlight, as opposed to daylight, because the light from a theater spotlight comes from only one discrete place, objects that interrupt this light cause shadows. The sky is different: Its light shines all around a figure. Light from the sky, as opposed to sunlight or light from a theatrical spotlight, is shadowless.

Here, the understanding and use of dominant and recessive colors can help create an illusion of daylight without re-creating a full surround of light to simulate the fill-in quality that results from the infinite angles of skylight. Recessive colors can be used to "fill in" the shadows caused by dominant colors in a lighting composition and act like the light from a sky or other multidirectional, ambient sources. The shadows from these lights can be diminished and obscured by the shadows of the more dominantly colored key light.

Here's a figure with only a single source of backlight turned on.

Illus. 10.11. An idea of sunlight.

Let's imagine that this light is sunlight on a bright afternoon. What is missing from this photograph? We need a simulation of daylight. Here is the figure with a recessive sky-blue light filling in the shadows of the dominant key light.

Illus. 10.12. Here we have the addition of fill light representing the light from the sky.

Sky-blue sidelight and front light fill in this picture of a person in the afternoon sun. The sunlight diagonal backlight is still dominant, yellow being a very dominant color, even against many more sources with recessive pale blues.

Earlier, I stated that less saturated colors tend to dominate more saturated colors. Here that statement is overridden by the dominance of yellow over the less saturated blue tones. All the factors to consider when determining which colors will be dominant and which will be recessive are relative to a composition.

Because the yellow backlight is meant to be sunlight, the blue light, standing in for daylight, is a shadow color or fill light, because it fills in the shadows of the primary light or key light.

> **Tip:** *When composing a lighting setup, try to start with the key light. Balance the other lights in the composition to that initial gesture.*

What is the story that you want to tell with this light? In this case, we want the viewer to believe that we are outside in the sunlight. The sunlight is the first thing that I will turn on. This is very important. But just as important is the color and angles of the shadow, or fill, light. With these choices, a designer can make a big statement about style and mood and place.

THE COLORS OF DAYLIGHT

What color is the daylight? It comes from the sun, so it follows that it is the same color as the sun. Or is it? Is there something in the atmosphere that filters the sunlight as it passes through all of the molecules of nitrogen, oxygen, and carbon dioxide? Daylight on a sunny clear day is sunlight. But because of a complex interactive relationship between the sizes and shapes of the molecules in the atmosphere and the sizes of the wavelengths of light present in sunlight, the light at the shorter end of the spectrum is scattered, while the light at the longer end of the spectrum passes through without as much scattering. This phenomenon is called "Rayleigh scattering," and it is responsible for making the sky blue (wavelengths at the shorter end of the spectrum). It is not that the atmosphere is a filter, letting only blue light pass; it is that some of the sunlight that would have passed us by overhead is captured and scattered by the atmosphere to light up the daytime sky.

At the beginning and end of the day, as the earth's rotation positions the sun not overhead but lower in the sky, sunlight passes through more atmosphere. Because of the increasing amount of atmosphere through which the light passes on its way to our eyes, the scattering effect increases, leaving the longer wavelengths for us to see at the red side of the spectrum. Because of Rayleigh scattering, the sun appears redder the closer it is to the horizon, giving dawns and dusks those warm pink and magenta hues.

When asked, many people would report that daylight is blue and sunlight is yellow. Apollo rides a golden chariot through the daytime sky. But at midday, when the sun passes through a relatively thin layer of atmosphere, sunlight is a full spectrum of white light, not yellow at all.

Rayleigh scattering gives us a blue sky and, at the end of a day, a golden sun, but there is something else going on here. Sunlight is not golden throughout the day, but ask a young child to draw the sun with a set of crayons and they will almost universally choose a yellow color. However, if you really look at sunlight on a clear day, it is decidedly not yellow. It is brighter than daylight and less blue, but usually not quite golden.

It can be quite difficult, though, to accurately reproduce the intensity range of sunlight and daylight on a stage, and like the limitation of drawing something as complex as the sun and the sky with a set of crayons on a white paper, a lighting designer can use color range to stand in for intensity range. In our mind's eye, we assign yellow to the sun and blue to the sky to be able to render the scene with a poetic fidelity. Understanding this color hierarchy is something that will inform your own choices when creating lighting compositions that communicate meaning to an audience.

CONCLUSION

Our brains are not equally sensitive to all the colors across the spectrum. This relative sensitivity has been plotted on a graph named the "luminosity function." In addition to this physiological preference, there are other color preferences that are based on culture as well as personal choice. These preferences together can be used to form a hierarchy of color within any given visual composition. Some colors are dominant and other colors are recessive. A visual artist can use this knowledge of dominant and recessive colors to help create compositions that articulate light and shadow, depth and brightness, in clear and effective ways.

Tip: *On a proscenium or end stage set, in addition to lighting a scene by starting with the key light, i.e., the most important system of light, try working by building each system from the back of the stage to the front. The great lighting designer Craig Miller used to say, "Front light should be thought of as salt and pepper on the table. It is to be added after the meal is cooked and used sparingly to taste." By arranging the compositional build this way, a designer can ensure that the key light retains its primacy. This method will also make it easier to build more dimensional compositions.*

PRACTICAL: CREATING DEPTH WITH COLOR

The arrangement of the colors from a palette within a lighting composition can have a major effect on the perceived depth of the figures that are being lit. Think about arranging the colors of a palette to increase the apparent depth of the composition.

As an exercise, set up the diagrammed lighting in your light lab as shown in Illustration 10.13. There are low sidelights on the figure, diagonal backlights, and a front light. In addition, the cyclorama is lit from the bottom.

Color the lights with the three palettes given below, or their mixed equivalent if you have LED fixtures. Try different arrangements of the colors within each palette while attempting to arrange the colors in order to maximize the feeling of depth in the compositions. Pick a recording of a song that you like for each palette and create cues that, for you, connect visually to the chosen song. Think about the possible relationships of color to music and how that might be transmitted to an audience.

PALETTE 1: Roscolux **27**, Roscolux **10**, Roscolux **316**, Roscolux **88**, Roscolux **90**

PALETTE 2: Roscolux **76**, Roscolux **16**, Roscolux **54**, Roscolux **64**, Roscolux **80**

PALETTE 3: Roscolux **33**, Roscolux **49**, Roscolux **79**, Roscolux **78**, Roscolux **48**

Illus. 10.13. Lighting setup for the Practical: plan and rendering.

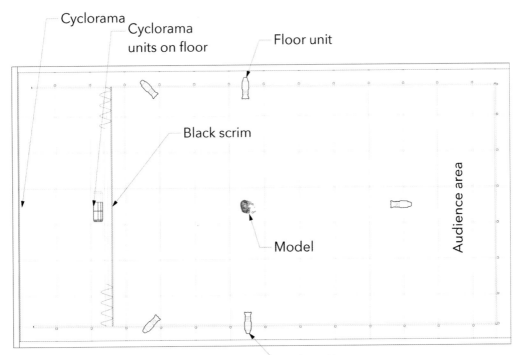

Cyclorama

Cyclorama
units on floor

Floor unit

Black scrim

Model

Audience area

Floor Unit

MONOCHROMATIC AND POLYCHROMATIC PALETTES

The concept of monochromatic and polychromatic lighting palettes was introduced in Chapter 9, on saturation. Let's get a better understanding of what is meant by these terms.

MONOCHROMATIC PALETTES ARE RADIUSES OF A COLOR SPACE

We work with monochromatic lighting palettes all the time. It is often the best choice for lighting a scene. A monochromatic palette does not necessitate that every light have exactly the same color (though that is possible and sometimes desirable). Individual lights in a monochromatic palette can have different colors. What distinguishes a monochromatic palette is that all of the colors could be charted along a straight line in the CIE color space that is a radius between a white point and a spectral color along the edge. A monochromatic palette can contain any color that falls along this line between the spectrum and white.

In Illustration 11.1, a line is drawn that connects a blue color on the edge of the color space with a white somewhere on the Kelvin line. (Any hue along the edge of the space can form the basis of

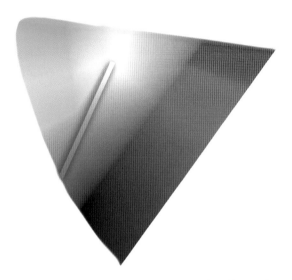

Illus. 11.1. The 1976 u'v' color space with a monochromatic line from blue to white.

a monochromatic palette, not just this blue.) The line represents a path of saturation.

Recall the demonstration of blue being desaturated with yellow from Chapter 9. Now consider this demonstration in terms of working with monochromatic palettes. As colors are desaturated along a radial line toward a white point, the white point occurs at a point just before the base color flips and starts to saturate toward the complement.

By increasing the amount of complementary color in our desired monochromatic palette, we eventually reach a point when the color tips and the composition becomes polychromatic.

A polychromatic flip can also occur if the colors diverge too far from the radial line. In this example, this would occur if a blue were introduced into the composition that had too much green in it or too much red in it compared with the other blues in the composition.

FINDING WHITE

In Chapter 8, on white light, we saw how a viewer will choose the least saturated color and assign it as the white in the composition. Our visual processing system will also seek to increase the apparent contrast ratio between the lightest and darkest colors in the palette. I think this capacity evolved to maximize the available information in what our eyes see. Our eyes are many times more capable across a range of lighting conditions to pick out details, find contrast, and see movement than any general-purpose camera system yet developed. This is possible because our brains adjust to the light input and adjust or shift the entire composition around this assigned color, assigning it to the white point position.

SEARCHING FOR A COMPLETE SPECTRUM

Polychromatic palettes increase the complexity of a visual composition. A viewer of a polychromatic composition will increase the contrast of the present colors. In the viewer's mind, colors will be pushed out toward the edges of the color space. Looking at any scene, our brain looks for a complete set of colors.

Whenever it is possible to do so, our brains will push colors out toward the edge of the color space in order to gain as much contrast information from a scene as possible. Even when a complete range of colors is not present in a composition, our vision systems have evolved the ability to try to increase the range of the existing colors. It is especially important to remember this tendency when working with pale colors.

CONCLUSION

A palette of lighting colors for a scene can be characterized as either a monochromatic or a polychromatic palette. The statements "a palette of pale blues" and "a palette of pinks" usually describe monochromatic palettes. In that mode, the viewer looks for differences in saturation contrast.

When looking at a polychromatic palette, the viewer will look for differences in hue contrast. Our visual system has a preference for polychromatic palettes over monochromatic palettes and will look for hue contrasts whenever possible. Since pale tints, i.e., colors near white in the color space, actually contain some amount of all spectral colors, it is very easy for a pale monochromatic palette to flip into being seen as a polychromatic palette.

Tip: *When a monochromatic palette flips into a polychromatic palette, it happens for one of two reasons. The first possibility is that one of the colors is not located along the radial line between the deepest spectral color and the white point of the color space. In that case, the solution is to find a substitute color that more closely fits to the line. The second possibility for the apparent polychromatic flip is that the palest color is perceived to be on the other side of the white point, i.e., it crosses over to the complementary side of the white point, onto the opposite radius. Increasing the saturation of the palest color in the palette, back toward the desired color, has the effect of lessening the quantity of complementary colors present in that color. In most cases the viewer will still assign the palest color as white, but the overall effect will be a cleaner monochromatic palette.*

PRACTICAL: DISCOVERING MONOCHROMATIC PALETTES

Start with these five colors: Lee 132, Roscolux 59, Lee 126, Roscolux 76, Roscolux 10. For each color, find five other gel colors that would form a monochromatic progression where the gel colors progress toward white in steps that are as evenly spaced as possible. Keep in mind the specific hues of the given colors, and try to maintain those hues in the new chosen colors.

Arrange your colors like the lighting setup shown in Illustration 11.2.

Does the palette appear monochromatic when looked at in light? What happens when you increase or add more of a certain color of lights in the composition? Does the composition retain its monochromatic quality?

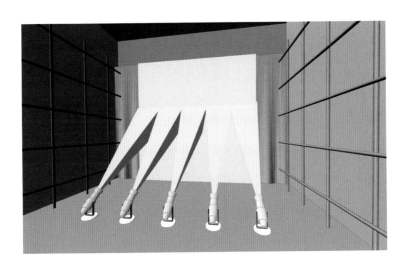

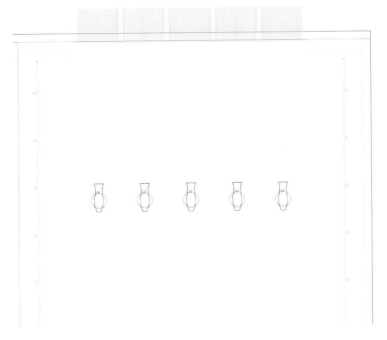

Illus. 11.2. Setup for monochromatic palette explorations.

COLOR RENDERING, LIMITED SPECTRUM SOURCES, AND NEW COLOR SPACES

Each source of light that we work with creates its own color space. It is not just that an arc source produces a subset of the tungsten color space, which is often how it is described. It is also important to realize that an arc source produces colors that are technically nearly impossible to reproduce with a tungsten source. The filters do not exist or would be very expensive to mass produce. It is even harder to go the other way (re-creating tungsten filtered colors with arc sources), because of the wavelengths that are missing from the source lamp. No amount of filtering will cause them to suddenly appear! It is very difficult to get an arc source to look like a tungsten on all of the varied surfaces where we project light.

Each source of light produces its own color space and offers the possibilities of creating unique color mixes that are not possible to create with any other source!

FULL SPECTRUM SOURCES

Sunlight, the light that our eyes evolved to detect, is a full spectrum source. The sun emits light across the visible range of frequencies on all wavelengths. Because all of the possible wavelengths of light within the visible spectrum are present, sunlight will reveal all possible visible local colors. Imagine a flower that has petals of a strange and specific color within the visible spectral range. No matter what that color is, sunlight hitting that flower will reflect it into our eyes and we will be able to see it.

A full spectrum source is one that produces all the wavelengths of visible light. Sunlight, moonlight, firelight, and Thomas Edison's electric light bulb are all full spectrum sources of white light. All of the wavelengths of visible light are output in each of these sources, though, and—this is critical—not in the same relative proportions. The difference can be described by looking at its spectral power distribution, or SPD graph.

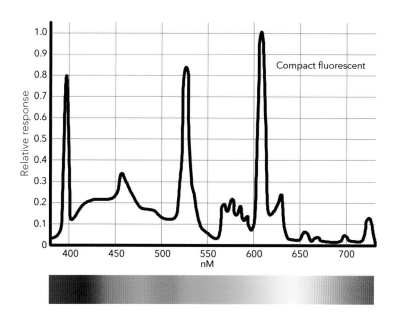

Illus. 12.1. Spectral output of a 14w Ecosmart Truecolor compact fluorescent lamp. Data source: *Popular Mechanics*.

Not all light sources are full spectrum sources. Many sources of light output a subset of the visible spectrum. Sometimes we can see this as a distinct color—a laser light or an LED emitter, for instance.

Because we do not have eyes with specific detectors for every wavelength in the visible spectrum, it is possible to simulate full spectrum white light with limited spectrum sources. For instance, we have LED and fluorescent light bulbs that simulate the light that comes from an incandescent household light bulb. In the beginning of this book, Newton's sketch of his refracting experiment was reproduced, in which he discovered that sunlight could be broken up into the component spectral colors. If we perform this same experiment with a limited spectrum source, refracting the light from an LED, arc, or fluorescent source, we will see that it does not produce a complete spectrum of light. The spectral power distribution (SPD) for these sources is spiky. Some wavelengths of light are missing.

LIMITED SPECTRUM SOURCES AND COLOR RENDERING

The limited spectral output of these sources limits the range of colors that can be rendered, or reflected by a surface or object. Even when a light appears to be white—as with an unfiltered arc source—there will be colors of fabrics or paint that do not, and cannot, appear correctly under that light. As we know, for a given paint or dye (local) color to be seen, it reflects the specific wavelengths of light that correspond to the local color and absorbs all of the other wavelengths. If the necessary wavelengths are not present in the light source, the local color has nothing to reflect and therefore the color will not be seen.

An extreme version of this can be seen in the sodium vapor street lighting of many cities. While sodium vapor sources, the yellowy-orange streetlights, are very power efficient, they are very poor color renderers because they output an extremely limited bandwidth of color frequencies. If you live in a place with sodium vapor streetlighting, go out at night and look at various colors of fabric under sodium vapor lights. Most colors cannot be seen under this light and the world becomes monochromatic. Shapes and shadows and a full range from light to darkness exist, but what of the greens and magentas of the sunlit world?

During the 20th century, when non–full spectrum sources came into common usage, the CIE developed a scale, called the Color Rendering Index or CRI, as an attempt to rate the white light quality of a given lamp. A full spectrum source has a CRI value of 100. Fluorescent and arc sources have different CRI numbers that are less than 100. The CRI has several deficiencies, however, and is being replaced by the newer, more rigorous standard for evaluating white light, TM-30-15 (which was mentioned in Chapter 8). Because CRI is a single number rating, there is nothing in the standard that says how a given lamp is a certain number, and in fact two lamps with very different spectral signatures can be given the same CRI number even though they render color in very different ways. According to the Illuminating Engineering Society's *Design Guide for Color and Illumination*, TM-30 is a new standard under consideration at the time of this writing. The TM-30 testing is based on a much wider reflective color data set than CRI. In addition, TM-30 result data describes how a white light source renders color: specifically, whether it will decrease or increase the saturation level of a local color. The data can be graphed to easily see which colors are distorted and whether the distortion is positive or negative.

In my career as a theatrical designer, CRI was never an important consideration. However, it has always been extremely important for architectural designers. Now, as we move into a world where all of our luminaires are non–full spectrum sources like LED or arc or fluorescent, understanding the problems and language of color rendering has become very important for everyone who works with light. TM-30, while outside the scope of this book, is an important step forward in increasing our ability to evaluate sources for our use.

DRIVEN BY POWER EFFICIENCY

Why would we use a light source with such limitations? There are several reasons, usually having to do with power consumption and brightness. More lumen output per watt of electric input led us to widespread adoption of HIDs (High Intensity Discharge Arc Lamps). Tungsten light wastes most of the energy input as dissipated heat loss; very little of the input power goes into light output. The search for more power-efficient lighting sources has driven most of the research in lighting since Edison's time.

But power consumption is not often the artist's first concern. In today's market, we have at our disposal thousands of filter choices. Why use a limited spectral light at all when we can limit a full spectral source like an incandescent light with a color filter?

For the answer, we must realize that efficiency can be thought of in two ways. The first, as with a sodium vapor source, is the engineering goal to deliver the greatest amount of light for the least amount of energy. The second turns this idea around and delivers more light for the same amount of power! And this second version of efficiency is what has happened with modern stage lighting fixtures.

CAN I SEE THAT AT 120%?

We have continually sought brighter and brighter sources, and it is safe to assert that most stage productions today are more brightly lit than in the past. First and foremost, it is our quest for brightness that has led to the widespread adoption of arc sources in the theater. When these first appeared, they usually remained unfiltered. I'm thinking of a single 10,000 watt HMI Fresnel that could be used to light a stage by itself or effectively "cut through" a fully lit stage of tungsten ellipsoidal. The cold blue-white of these beautiful lights was enough of a statement.

Illus. 12.2. Laila Robins in Red Bull Theater's production of August Strindberg's *Dance of Death*. The final scene was lit with additional arc-sourced lamps, abstracting the realistic interior set. Directed by Joe Hardy. Scenery by Beowulf Boritt. Costumes by Alejo Vietti. Lighting by Clifton Taylor. Photograph by Beowulf Boritt.

THE REVOLUTION OF MOVING LIGHTS

Arc lights next appeared in moving lights, and it was here that color really came up as an issue. Moving lights (automated luminaires that can be programmed to reposition themselves with a lighting console) came into use as a tool in the touring concert world. Their adoption by theatrical designers was delayed for two reasons. First, they were relatively expensive and required a specialized control computer that was foreign to the world of the theater, and second, their color, both as an unfiltered source and with the early available color-mixing systems, was not seen as compatible with filtered tungsten stage light.

Many people saw this light as harsh and unforgiving to performers, scenery, and costumes. In addition, the early moving lights were noisy and required specialized power and control cabling. Each of these concerns was eventually addressed, of course, and today moving lights with arc sources exist in the lighting plots of almost every show on Broadway and throughout the performing arts.

Broadway is not limited to moving lights or any one type of lighting technology. The great lighting designer Natasha Katz lit the successful musical Once *with only a few moving lights in a very controlled and spare color palette. On Broadway in 2017, the play* Farinelli and the King *was fantastically lit with real candles and a few tungsten lights to support them by the lighting designer Paul Russell.*

The best current-technology lights are quite sophisticated, having smooth dousing systems that mimic a dimming curve very well and color-mixing engines internal to the lights calibrated with the ability to mix colors that are more compatible with a tungsten-keyed environment.

That said, as this is a book about color, it is important to understand that while we can get colors that are pretty close to a tungsten ellipsoidal with a filter from a color-mixing arc light, it is not the same and it actually cannot be the same.

THE ARTISTIC TAKE ON THIS

As artists, this is extremely interesting for us, because it means that each source gives us access to a new color space. It's not that one particular color space is superior to another. In fact, a color has no intrinsic value. Colors only have possible value in the context of a composition, and for theatrical designers, in the context of a story.

It might seem, when looking at the full range of color filters that are available today, that everything is covered! Or when reading a manufacturer's marketing materials for a new luminaire that can produce a billion colors, one might think that that is certainly enough. But the truth is that the colors that an arc-sourced moving light can produce are different from the colors that can be made with filters on a fluorescent cool white light lamp, which are again very different from the possible colors of a filtered tungsten-based stage light.

So, instead of getting wrapped up in finding colors equiva-lent to those made with one kind of light, perhaps it would be interesting to explore what new colors are possible with various sources of light.

***Tip:** There are many conversion filters on the market that attempt to convert one type of light source to the color properties of another. While these filters in many cases go a long way to pushing one kind of light to mimic another, they will usually only work in very controlled circumstances and are more helpful in the context of film and television production, where the viewer (a camera) is much less sensitive to color variation than is the human eye. By all means, though, experiment with these filters and use them when you find it appropriate.*

THE MARCH OF TECHNOLOGY

In the 21st century, we're used to the idea that new technology displaces older technology. Thomas Edison's incandescent light replaced gaslight. Compact fluorescent bulbs have gone a far way to replacing incandescent lamps, and LED household bulbs are now replacing those.

Along this path we have learned to see differently. The colors that we see under compact fluorescent lighting are actually different and the change is as radical as the developments in fabrics and dyes that have accompanied the change in lighting. Today we produce fabric colors, like fluorescent green, that were not possible to make in the 20th century. Similarly, we can create colors of light today that could not have been produced in the recent past.

But remember the colors from the past. Think of how sepia is associated with the 19th and early 20th centuries because of the technology of photography. Think of how the color palettes made possible by Technicolor are associated with the middle of the 20th century. Just like a costume designer or a set designer, lighting designers can use the history of color to communicate the feeling of places and time periods. This is to be celebrated, because the story of color in paint and dye and light is the history of a culture.

An office fixture with tubes of fluorescent light is associated with the mid-20th century. A street bathed in mercury vapor light speaks of the 1970s. Someone manipulating the color of an LED light bulb with her smartphone puts us into the 2010s. Color pigments also have their own history. The cost and rarity of certain pigments have determined their relative use in paintings in different points in our history. The newly available pigments during the Italian Renaissance fundamentally changed the nature of painting. The history of blue pigments over the ages, from the ultramarine of ground-up lapis lazuli to the synthetic pigments of the 20th century, shows us how a color can change our understanding of a culture.

I remember a time on Broadway in the mid-1980s when strong indigo beams of light first became possible. This was because the sources that were available became bright enough to push enough light through a glass indigo filter so that it could be seen and used as a source of light. Indigo light became fashionable. And this fashion was driven by the newly available technology of an arc source luminaire, a limited spectrum source that could output a lot of indigo light.

BUT WHAT IF I DON'T CARE ABOUT EFFICIENCY?

If brightness and efficiency were not an issue, would there be a reason to want to use a limited spectrum source? Think about a piano keyboard. If the 88 keys are the full spectrum of light, then white light is the equivalent of playing all the notes at once. A laser light is like playing just one note. Perhaps a limited spectrum source could be thought of as equivalent to playing only the notes that exist in one key. As an example, the key of C encompasses only the white keys on the piano. You would still hear the full range of the instrument from lowest to highest, but there would be something missing, and the missing parts in fact yield a new understanding of the spectrum.

In music, the missing notes lead to a universe of feeling and emotional meaning. Certain kinds of music lend themselves to certain keys, and the keys are by no means equivalent. Perhaps it is similar with color. Are there colors available in the color spaces of limited spectrum sourced luminaires that resonate a feeling that is not easily accessed in a full spectrum color space?

"[B]ut what counts most is the intervals between colors, precisely chosen."—David Salle, How to See

CONCLUSION

When a new light source comes into use, usually the first question asked is, "How can it be integrated into the existing ideas about color, control, and intensity?" A lot of engineering work has gone into developing the hardware and software tools to make the light from a Vari-Lite 3500 moving light look just like an ETC Source Four when the need arises. Less has been written about the unique color space of the VL3500 or any of the other tools that are now available. In my own work, I know that there is usually not enough time in the theater—during technical rehearsals—to really explore the color possibilities of each light.

As lighting designers, we are expected to come to a lighting session knowing the solutions before we turn on a light, and that is becoming more and more difficult because of the explosion of different sources and LED color engines that have become available. I spent many years exploring the color space created by tungsten-based theatrical lights filtered with color media. This color space has been more or less standard for more than 70 years. It took almost 20 years to fully integrate the use of arc sources with internal subtractive color-mixing systems into wide-spread use in the theater. Now LED luminaires, each with their own component colors, color engines—and therefore unique color spaces—are appearing nearly every month.

Most of these LED fixtures have differing color capacities. Is the LED light using three colors, four colors, or seven colors? Is it designed for warm palettes, soft palettes, white palettes, or every-thing? Each of these luminaires occupies its own color space, and there are color possibilities in an ETC Selador cyc (cyclorama) light that are completely different from a Color Kinetics wash luminaire. Be open to the possibility that each new fixture type may yield surprises and subtleties.

Tip: When working in situations where you are blending multiple sources—arc, LED, and tungsten—it will be helpful to take some time before technical rehearsals begin to try and match all of the filter colors in the show's lighting palette. You may have other uses planned for the color-mixing units, but start out by creating custom palettes for your colors so that when you are under time pressure, you will be able to call upon colors that you know will work together. Having these palettes already made, you will be able to work much more efficiently during pressured rehearsals.

PRACTICAL: MIXING TUNGSTEN AND NON-TUNGSTEN SOURCES

In a light lab, point a tungsten-sourced stage light at a mannequin from one side. From the opposite side, point an HMI source at the mannequin.

Ideally, the two sides of the mannequin should be lit with equal intensity.

Adjust the intensity of the HMI source with a mechanical douser (either one that is internal to the fixture or one that is an external device attached to the fixture). Now, with filter(s) on the tungsten fixture, try to match the color of the HMI fixture.

Were you able to do this? What happens when you change costumes on the figure? What happens if you lower the intensity of the two sources? Does the color stay matched during the fade?

13.

REVISITING DOMINANT AND RECESSIVE COLORS

WHAT IS BRIGHTER THAN WHITE?

In Chapter 10, on color dominance, I posited that our brains prioritize colors and order them according to that priority. Imagine a scene that is lit with all-white (tungsten) light. Is there a color that is more dominant than all of that white? For instance, perhaps the scene is all white, but you need a backlight to help push the figures visually forward in the space.

What could work? Well, there are a few choices. Yellow, something like Roscolux 10, could work that way, or a pale green, like Roscolux 88. Why are these colors more dominant than white that contains all spectral colors? The answer is in the balance of the component parts. Roscolux 10 filters out some of the blue of a white light, and Roscolux 88 filters out some of the lavender. Both rebalance white light so that it contains less of the most recessive colors, so when compared with unfiltered white light, they both have the potential to dominate.

BECOME AN ANALYST OF COLORS

For theater lighting designers it is often necessary to solve problems very quickly. The practice of defining dominant and recessive colors within a composition will help you to understand why a color palette is or is not working.

Similarly, it is increasingly important to be able to look at a color of light onstage and imagine how it is being made. What are the component parts of that color? With color-mixing luminaires, you are able to manipulate a color to move toward dominance or recessiveness by manipulating the filters or emitters that are creating the color.

Let's say that you had created the all-white composition described at the beginning of this chapter. Now you need to push the backlight color toward a more dominant color to help visually separate the performers from the scenery. In the past, we might have done exactly what I described, put Roscolux 88 into the clear backlight system. But with a color-mixing luminaire in the backlight position, it is more important to know that reducing the amount of lavender or blue in the backlight will achieve the effect of pushing the figure forward.

What used to be solved by memorizing the available filter numbers—and sometimes frantically searching through swatch books at the design table, looking for a solution to a problem at hand—is now an action at the console that manipulates the color of the light. This can be tricky because you have to know how the color is being created to be able to take effective action.

On a subtractive three-color-mixing arc source, to reduce the lavender you might reduce the level of the magenta and cyan flags. On a four-color-mixing LED light, you might increase the green LED. On a seven-color-mixing LED light, you could take one of many actions to achieve an acceptable result.

LIGHTING COLOR AND LOCAL COLOR

Light reveals things—figures, objects, and sometimes space. The colors with which we work have no intrinsic meaning except that they fall onto actors, dancers, costumes, and scenery. Fabric and paint have local colors of pigments and dyes. For these colors to be revealed, they must receive the specific wavelengths of light that will be reflected off those pigments and dyes. A solid red piece of cloth absorbs green and blue wavelengths of light; it only reflects red wavelengths of light. Therefore, if we want to see the red of the cloth, we have to project onto it that specific red wavelength of light.

Here is the tricky part, though: Is the red cloth the only thing in the scene? Perhaps the red cloth is made into a skirt that is worn by an actress, who is also wearing a purple robe and a golden crown. Behind the figure is a large tapestry of many colors. How, then, do you choose colors for the light that will work with all of these local colors?

Remember that as we move a color to the center of a color space we are adding all of the other colors from the spectrum into that color. So, all of the colors near the center of a color space, the color circle or a CIE color space, contain some or all of the colors in the spectrum.

Imagine now a similar red costume, only this one is made up of 20 different reds, all deep jewel-like tones but all subtly different from each other. What kind of light would make this costume the most vivid thing possible? A deep red light projected onto this costume would certainly give all those reds something to reflect, but would it minimize or maximize the differences in the local colors of the costume? In this example, a very saturated red light, made up of very few different wavelengths of light, would minimize the diversity in this complex costume. All of the subtleties of the different reds would be lost!

To understand this, let's look at how the fabric's different reds are created. To make 20 different red dyes you would need to manipulate the basic red dye with small amounts of other colors. Add a little yellow to one, a little green to another, and a little blue to a third. These 20 reds actually contain small amounts of many other colors! It is important for the lighting designer to provide those other wavelengths of light so that the subtleties can be seen.

The trick for a lighting designer is to find the right balance between providing all of the necessary wavelengths of light so that all of the local colors can be seen, and creating a visual language of lighting color that can take on meaning in the context of the theatrical event.

Up until now, we've talked about dominant and recessive colors only in terms of lighting. But the idea must be extended to the entire visual composition. It is possible for a lighting color to overwhelm the local color palette of a costume or set piece. This can be because the lighting color is too saturated in comparison with the complexity of the lit subject. But it also can be because of hue considerations alone. A yellow key light could dominate the dress of pale blue colors. A magenta follow spot could improperly dominate the firebird costume of a hundred different red feathers.

CONCLUSION

The language of dominant and recessive color creates a way of thinking about color relationships that can help you choose colors for a scene and also arrange those colors in the light plot. Any two colors will have a dominant and recessive relationship, and you can use that relationship to communicate ideas about the space, mood, style, and time of day for the scene that you are lighting, in addition to solving problems that may arise when you're looking at a lighting composition.

With color-mixing luminaires, this idea can also help you to mix color for a scene as you're looking at it. Ask yourself if the backlight color would work better if it were more dominant. Would the fill or front light color blend better if it were a more recessive hue? Is it possible to change the sense of depth in the scene by affecting the color of the cyclorama or scenery?

PRACTICAL: WORKING WITH SCENERY AND COSTUMES

EXERCISE

Set up the lights in your lab following the plan shown in Illustrations 13.1 and 13.2. Dress a model or mannequin in a variety of red, maroon, and orange colors.

Choose a pink-to-magenta color palette for the lights that makes all of the colors work together in a way that you like. Is there a level of saturation that makes it more difficult to appreciate the differences in the costume?

What happens if you manipulate the color of the light toward more reds and oranges (dominant colors)?

What happens if you move the color of the light toward more blues and lavenders (recessive colors)?

Experiment with saturated and unsaturated color palettes to find the right balance between the color of the light and the rendition of the local colors of the costume.

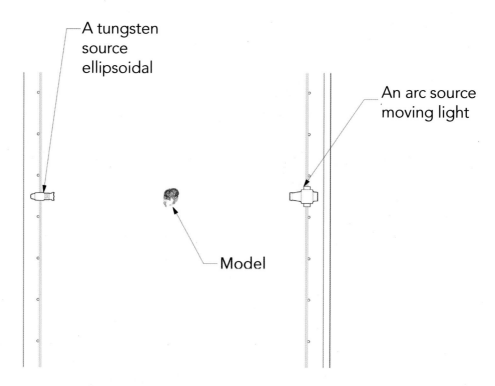

A tungsten source ellipsoidal

An arc source moving light

Model

Illus. 13.1. Plan for lighting setup for the practical.

Illus. 13.2. Rendering of lighting setup for the practical.

COLOR & LIGHT

14.

DIMMING, DOUSING, AND REDSHIFT

When we dim a filament-based fixture, the white light output from the lamp shifts down on the Kelvin scale. This effect is called a *redshift*. It is a result of the technology of tungsten lamps and dimming. If you work with dimming lamps, your eyes come to expect this shift, and if you are around it a lot, it becomes a natural part of what you expect a light to do. It is, after all, a natural part of how firelight works: As a fire cools down, the color of the light shifts to warmer and warmer hues. This effect is not apparent just when a light is near zero on a dimming curve but also at higher levels, and, it can be noted, especially in pale colors, even when a unit is dimmed from 100% to 80%.

REDSHIFT IN TUNGSTEN/INCANDESCENT FIXTURES AND HOW COLORS ARE AFFECTED

A tungsten-based light filtered through a piece of Roscolux 54 Pale Lavender outputs a different color when it is full than when it is at 80%. In fact, each level of output implies a different color space for the source lamp. Most of the time, we choose color with the idea or assumption that the source lamp will be at full. Many problems in color composition arise when a tungsten lamp isn't used at full and the resulting color is not what you expected.

This is especially true with very pale colors. As a lamp is dimmed lower and lower, the redshift effect grows stronger and stronger, and many times this effect overwhelms the color filter so that it makes little difference at 20% if the light has a Roscolux 53 filter or a Roscolux 54 (both pale lavender) filter.

Tip: If you find that a lamp is consistently used at a low level and its color is problematic, consider shifting its color filter to compensate for the redshift. Choose a filter color with more cyan in it (the lighting complement of red) to help counteract the redshift, or use a neutral-density filter to lower the output of the light without altering its color, to be able to use it at a higher dimmer level.

MECHANICAL DOUSING

Arc sources are not dimmable in the same way as a filament source. A theatrical arc-sourced luminaire stays on for the entire show. To achieve the effect of dimming and to control the relative intensity of the luminaire, a mechanical douser is used. In some cases, the douser is external to the luminaire, as with film-industry–type HMI Fresnels, while in others it is built into the unit, as with most modern arc-based moving lights.

Mechanical dousers have come a long way, and now the best ones can reliably simulate a dimming curve even at very low levels. However, because of the absence of redshift, the color path these units take as they are "dimming out" is not the same as that of a tungsten-based luminaire.

In the film, television, and photographic industries, this is usually desirable. Redshift is a natural by-product of dimming a filament-based source, but the effect introduces more color problems for the camera than it does for a live audience in the theater. You will rarely find dimmers being used in lighting setups made for cameras. The preferred method has been to filter a source with scrims (metal window screening material) or neutral density filters. This is done so that you can manipulate the intensity of a source while preserving the agreed-upon white point to which the cameras are balanced. Our eyes are constantly adjusting the white point of everything that we see. Cameras are not that nimble!

SIMULATING REDSHIFT

In the theater, because it has been the technology that we have had and because it has a connection to the natural world of fire and sunlight, redshift has been embedded into the way that we have seen light for more than a century. Every bit of lighting design that incorporates tungsten lights has dealt with redshift in some way—so much so that it has become normalized. But as we move into more and more situations without tungsten luminaires, we see that it is a unique property of these lights, and, going forward, it will not necessarily be the default choice for how a light behaves as it is being faded in or out.

Luminaires with mechanical dousers, dimming fluorescents, and LED sources do not inherently redshift along with intensity changes. Until now, in many theatrical situations where we had mixed tungsten and arc sources, we have tended to ignore the problem caused when some of the equipment redshifts and some does not. I have on a few occasions manipulated a color-mixing moving light to increase the red as the light dims, but it has been a tedious and time-consuming process, and it is rare in the theater to have the time to work with this level of precision. But it can be done, and sometimes it is essential to the look that all the lights appear to dim in the same way.

I don't think that there is something inherently good or bad about redshifting. It is something that film and television lighting directors have had to work around. I know many television designers are happy to have LED-based luminaires in their toolbox precisely because this technology frees them from the problems of redshift. But I also know that the redshifting is built into the lighting designs that were built around tungsten equipment, and when we move into a space that only has LED gear, we will need good solutions for simulating this effect accurately so that we can see what the lighting designers of the 20th and early 21st centuries intended. Software is beginning to be developed to simulate redshift automatically within certain LED-sourced luminaires, though as with all simulations, you could argue about its fidelity to the original design intent.

BUT WILL WE CARE IN THE FUTURE?

Perhaps redshift's importance will diminish as dimmer-controlled tungsten lights go out of use. Redshift simulation in LED-based lights is something that I care about now because, at this writing, we are in a transitional state across the lighting world. Already in the theater, we are used to looking at many arc sources that do not redshift, and we have made the collective visual adjustment that this can be "normal."

THE DIMMING CURVE

Apart from the question of redshift is the problem of dimming with non-incandescent sources. Dimming is something that is fundamental to the manipulation of light for performance, and our perception of a color is intimately connected to the intensity of a light. A whole world of engineering and infrastructure investment has gone into the development and deployment of dimmers to control tungsten-based luminaires in the theater. The ability to dim a source of light, either through mechanical, electrical, or electronic means, is the most important prerequisite to its widespread adoption as a tool for use in the professional theater or studio. This has been less true in the film and television industries because most of the dramaturgical functions of dimming in the theater are usually taken over by the camera. But in the theater, dimming is an essential function.

Most of the technical problems of simulating a dimmer curve (intensity path), whether by a mechanical douser or electronically, appear at the lowest end of the dimmer's curve. Especially with LED sources, it is very difficult to smooth out the path from 0% to 20%, and many, especially less expensive, lights have visible steps when they transition through each percentage level. Unlike redshift, it is difficult to imagine a time when smooth dimming would not be important to the way that we want to light a scene or a play, so further developments in simulated dimming will be most welcome.

BLACKOUTS, AFTERGLOW, PREHEATING, AND STROBE EFFECTS

Incandescent-type sources work by heating a filament until it outputs light. When you remove power from the filament, there is a period of time while the filament is cooling that it is still emitting light. Especially with high-wattage lamps, this means that it is sometimes very difficult to get a zero-count blackout. Similarly, there is a "ramp-up" time built into the way that filaments need to heat up before they can begin to output light. If you want to get a tungsten-sourced light to full in a zero count, sometimes it makes sense to pre-heat the instrument to a very low level, so that the filament is already hot and emitting a very small amount of light before you need it at full. This will make the ramp-up time shorter and the lights will appear to turn on faster.

Mechanical systems in moving lights with so-called "strobing shutters" can be faster than this filament heat-up or cool-down time, so in a mixed fixture environment, sometimes you must work to manage the relative times of a fade between instrument types so that all the lights appear to be working together. This is especially true of LED equipment. It is extremely good at instantaneous on and off switching, and it can be quite thrilling to see a stage "turn on" or "blackout" with true zero timing. LEDs make great strobes for this reason.

CONCLUSION

Each form of lighting technology comes with inherent features and limitations. Tungsten lights redshift when they are dimmed and because of their inherent properties will not strobe on and off instantly. Arc units do not dim from zero to full, but can, through mechanical means, be made to appear to do so. LEDs, natural strobing devices, can be made to simulate a tungsten dimmer curve as well as a redshift, though it is important to remember that this is a simulation and not equivalence. To simulate a tungsten source's dimmer curve precisely with an LED source, you have to consider both redshift and the specific light output at each point of the dimmer curve. At the same time, a tungsten-based lighting instrument cannot simulate the instantaneous color changing or strobing possibilities of LED fixtures currently on the market. They are different technologies, each with its own strengths and limitations. None is a direct substitute for the other.

PRACTICAL: SIMULATING REDSHIFT

Set up three ellipsoidal lights in your light lab: one unfiltered tungsten-based Source Four ellipsoidal, one LED-based ellipsoidal in a mode where you have access to all the emitters and redshift is turned off, and finally one LED-based fixture in a mode with native redshift turned on, if that is available.

Focus the lights so that they create three rectangles on a white wall with the sides of the rectangles touching each other.

Create nine cues where the three lights are at 100%, 75%, 50%, 35%, 25%, 15%, 10%, 5%, and off.

In each cue, try to match the LED lights to the tungsten source in terms of intensity and color. Record the results on the form for recording mixed colors from Appendix B.

What did you have to do to make this happen? How did the modes on the two LED sources affect how you programmed for each dimmer level?

See the complexities in simulating a tungsten source.

Try this again with a color such as Lee 161. Is it easier with a colored source?

15.

ADDITIVE MIXING REVISITED IN A WORLD OF LEDs

Lighting designers have been on an ongoing quest for a better color-changing light since the advent of stage lighting. In the beginning of our collective exploration of stage light, there was of course the additive color mixing of using more than one fixture pointed at the same focus area. We see this in three- and four-cyclorama strip lights and double- or triple-hung backlight or sidelight systems, where color is mixed by adding the light from two or more differently colored lights. In many cases this works quite well. But there has also been a long-term quest to find single sources that could change color. Indexing mechanical color wheels were the first such systems, followed by scrollers that change a filter on a light through a computer-controlled mechanical system.

COLOR-FADING MECHANICAL SYSTEMS

After this technology became available, several manufacturers came up with double- and triple-scrolling devices that allowed for variable subtractive color mixing. Morpheus's M-Faders (later superseded by the much more effective and versatile S-Fader line) and Wybron's CXI were competing products that enabled color mixing to come into widespread use. Concurrent with these developments, the moving light manufacturers were perfecting three- and four-color-mixing systems using dichroic glass chips that could be variably inserted into the beam of light within a fixture. This technology was later introduced into a fixed luminaire form via Ocean Optics SeaChangers and Wybron's Nexera model fixtures, among others.

THE BLUE LED EMITTER

With the invention of the blue LED, the dream of a non-mechanical additive color-mixing fixture became possible, and manufacturers have painstakingly worked out the optics so that framing profile or ellipsoidal-like luminaires based on an LED-emitter engine with full color-mixing capabilities have become widely available in both fixed focus and moving light form factors. The LED-based fixtures have many advantages over earlier mechanical systems. First, they are solid-state with no moving parts. This is a practical advantage in the entertainment industry, where equipment is packed and trucked, sometimes on a daily basis, and mechanical systems are especially difficult to maintain. Second, they reduce the heat and power load requirements for the facilities in which they are installed, as well as make it possible to reduce the infrastructure costs of dimming and heavy power distribution.

But let us leave these issues aside and consider the advent of the LED into the world of lighting solely from the point of view of color. First and foremost, remember that LEDs are additive color-mixing luminaires. There is no such thing as a default white light in the context of an LED color-mixing luminaire. If the light can output something that is similar to a tungsten or arc-sourced white, it is because there is an engineered recipe of component colored LEDs that create the desired white light. It is not, and never will be, equivalent to a full spectrum source. This engineered solution is getting better and better with each generation. In the highest-end luminaires we are seeing better facsimiles of tungsten light.

ADDITIVE COLOR: CHANGING THE IDEA OF SATURATION AND INTENSITY

LED-based additive color mixing luminaires change the relationship between intensity and saturation. With these fixtures, more saturated colors can exceed the output intensity of less saturated colors from the same fixture. This is an entirely new way to think about color because, through experience gained by using filtered tungsten sources, there is a parallel relationship of color saturation and intensity. With LEDs, and any additive color-mixing system, it is possible that there is an inverse relationship between saturation and intensity, or possibly no relationship, depending on the particulars of the component colors used in the fixture.

With subtractive color manipulation, we are used to thinking of intensity and color as two separate ideas. Color is something that has been applied to a light, not something that is, in fact, intrinsic to it. LED lights, and all additive color systems, force this initial misunderstanding to disappear. You cannot turn on a polychromatic LED source without making a decision about color. In terms of the computer control of an LED source, intensity is merely a function that is applied to the color palette output of the light.

The management and documentation of intensities, as was done with track sheets and other archival paperwork and computer files, gets much more complicated with LED fixtures than it was with dimmer-based fixtures or even arc-based moving lights. With color-mixing LED luminaires, there is not an assumed default white or default intensity upon which all of the colored light on a stage or in a picture depends. Each LED fixture type occupies its own color space, and not only is it difficult to simulate a tungsten fixture with an LED source, it can also be challenging to match one LED source to another.

LEDs ARE NARROW-BAND EMITTERS OF LIGHT

Like a laser that emits just one wavelength of light, i.e., just one color, individual LEDs emit light along very narrow bands of wavelengths (more or less 30nM per color). Over the years, LEDs have been engineered with fluorescent coatings to emit wider bandwidths of light, so that today there are LEDs that emit what can appear to be white light (which is accomplished either through a mixture of a blue LED and a warm, yellow color resulting from fluorescence or multiple LED emitters in a single source).

Mixing different color LED emitters to create other colors works quite well, just like when it was standard practice to use two or more colored tungsten sources to mix different colors additively. However, the devil is in the details! The earliest LED luminaires that were available commercially combined red, green, and blue emitters into a fixture. But these fixtures had several problems that prevented widespread adoption for general use in the professional theater beyond lighting scenery.

BUT DON'T RED, GREEN, AND BLUE MIX TO WHITE LIGHT?

Our eyes and vision systems are very complex. The cone cells are not such narrow detectors and they overlap in the range of color wavelengths to which they respond. These different kinds of color-detecting cells, along with the processing of visual information that our brains accomplish, make it impossible to simulate the experience of the full visible color space with just the three narrow bands of inputted light.

The complexities of local color that we can see depend on the full spectrum of light to tell their color stories. A subtle blush of personal recognition, the explosion of greens in a springtime forest, or the darkening sky of a gathering storm requires more nuance of lighting color to render than what is possible to create with a three-wavelength emitter.

TOWARD CREATING A LARGER COLOR SPACE

To help correct the problem of rendering colors on the outside edge of the full spectrum color space, makers of color-mixing LED lights have added additional LED color emitters to their fixtures. It is common to see fixture variations with added amber (RGBA) and/or white (RGBW or RGBAW) emitters. There are other systems on the market with seven color emitters, so this is not a settled issue. The increase in the number of colors within a luminaire is an attempt at achieving both the highest range of colors and also the best and brightest tungsten "white" simulation possible. Over the past 20 or so years of this development, the component colors of LEDs have shifted, due to both manufacturing availability and our collective project in learning about what has worked and what has not worked in the past. We are still at the beginning of this development.

SIMULATING A BETTER WHITE LIGHT

As we have seen, mixing red, green, and blue light alone can form a version of white light, but for rendering really complex colors, for instance skin tones, it is often less than satisfying. A performer's skin tone changes moment-to-moment with infinitely complex variation. An RGB fixture cannot render this subtlety with any kind of satisfying fidelity. I wouldn't recommend a fixture that didn't have at least four component colors, like RGBA or RGBW.

Lime green, while not a primary color, is on the spectrum. Our vision systems are extremely attuned to its presence in a color of light (the luminosity function) and it creates color dominance. Our sensitivity to lime-green light plays a big role in our perception of the color of the light.

IT'S NOT ONLY THE LIME GREEN THAT IS MISSING

The blue emitter in the LED array of a given luminaire defines the limit of colors that can be mixed on the spectrum from blue toward ultraviolet (UV). Wavelengths of light that approach UV are extremely important to our vision systems. It is these wavelengths that make possible magenta and indigo colors. When working in an additive system, it can be difficult to achieve lively magenta and indigo colors only by mixing red and blue primaries. Remember that in a subtractive system this is more easily achieved because these wavelengths of light are already present in the source. In an additive luminaire, like an LED-based ellipsoidal spotlight, if the color is not present in the source, it won't be projected by the light.

Some experiments have been done by shifting the blue emitter in a three- or four-color system toward indigo, but the problem with this method is that it makes it difficult to achieve a rich primary blue. A very purple-blue secondary color emitter mixed with a primary green emitter will create a color that moves away from the spectrum toward the center of the color space. Also remember that any secondary color mixed with any primary will yield a version of white light.

The answer, then, to rendering magentas, indigos, and blues properly is that there should be a primary blue emitter and an indigo emitter in the light. Indigo, like the lime green discussed earlier, is very important for opening a whole range of colors and tonalities that are not available in three- or four-color LED fixtures. It is an extremely recessive color hue and therefore can be slipped into a color recipe to enliven pinks and reds and purples as well as giving a flush to skin tones.

CONCLUSION

Because multicolor LED-based luminaires are additive color-mixing systems, there is no assumed relationship between intensity and color saturation. This change in how we think about color and light, from a world where color is applied to a light to one where color is the light, will have revolutionary implications going forward. With LEDs, white light, being simulated, becomes a choice for each cue instead of each fixture or each show. Each LED-based "color engine" occupies a unique color space, which will always be a subset of the full spectrum color space. For designs that must be re-created in other theaters after an original production lit with LED equipment, how will we document the chosen colors and intensities from the original cues? How will it be possible to re-create these designs with different fixtures in the future?

Tip: Mixing Color in an LED Luminaire

In LED equipment, intensity is a mathematical scalar function of the color palette. In other words, since there is no such thing as a dimmer for these lights, the intensity parameter of the channel acts on the color palette. When the light is set to "full," the computer looks at the color palette of the luminaire and outputs those values for each of the emitters. Any value less than full acts as a multiplier on the color palette, so that an intensity value of 80% will take each of the parameters of the color palette and multiply it by 0.8, and so on.

Therefore, if there is not at least one emitter set at full in a given color palette, the luminaire will never be able to achieve its full potential brightness in that color. With current lighting consoles that are dependent on the DMX protocol, we cannot set the value of an intensity channel above 100% or a scaling factor above 1.0.

There may be times when it's best to limit the output of the light through the programming of the color palette. When one is trying to simulate another unit type, it may be advantageous to limit the upper value of output within the color palette data to make older track sheets make better sense. However, for most situations when you are creating a new production, it is recommended to program the brightest version of the color possible in the color palette memory.

This is also true for luminaires with subtractive CMY color-mixing systems, and it can be useful in terms of having access to the greatest range of brightness for any programmed color, to make sure that at least one of the three or four flags is set to 0% or open for a given color palette.

PRACTICAL: PROGRAMMING COLOR WITH ADDITIVE AND SUBTRACTIVE SYSTEMS

Set up three lights in your light lab: one unfiltered tungsten-based ellipsoidal, one LED-based ellipsoidal in a mode where you have access to all the emitters and redshift is turned off, and finally one arc-based moving light (preferably a spot unit with shutters) with variable color control using dichroic color flags.If you can, focus the lights so that they are three rectangles on a white wall with the sides of the rectangles touching each other.

1. First, match the color and apparent intensity across all three lights on the wall.
2. Second, filter the tungsten ellipsoidal with Lee 142.
3. Now, using direct control over the emitters and the color flags in the moving light, match the Lee 142 color and intensity on the other two fixtures. Record the results on a form as in Appendix B.

For the LED fixture, what did you have to do to change the light to Lee 142? For the moving light, what did you have to do? How is this experience fundamentally different between the two fixture types?

16.

COLOR PATHS REVISITED

The idea of color paths was introduced back in Chapter 5 (The Color Circle and Color Spaces). From the advent of color-mixing luminaires, it has been desirable to be able to manipulate the color path that a fixture takes as it transitions from one color to another. The default action of a control console has been to fade each color element along a linear path during the time of the color fade. This approach results in one specific type of color path that sometimes is not visually desirable.

Here is an example: Fade a three-color subtractive moving light from blue to a sunny yellow. Create the blue by mixing cyan at full and magenta at full. Remember that, starting with white light, cyan filters out the red and magenta filters out the green, leaving us with blue light. Create a second cue where the yellow is made by yellow at full and cyan at 30% to make it a cooler yellow.

Without manipulating the fade times, when the light transitions from blue to yellow here is what will happen: The magenta flag will transition from full to 0. The yellow flag will transition from 0 to full. The cyan flag will transition from full to 30%. During this fade, it is possible that one might see more green light than is desirable.

The color path just described is completely different visually from the color path that would occur if there were two separate fixtures, one with a saturated blue filter like Roscolux 80 and the other with a yellow filter like Lee 101, and with dimmers faded from the blue light to the yellow light. This color path is different from one in which an LED fixture faded from a cue where the blue emitters were at full and the green emitters were at a lower level to simulate Roscolux 80, to a cue where the red and the green emitters are at a mixture that simulates the Lee 101.

Visually, these three fades will look completely different and in fact follow different color paths. Even within a fixture type, it is possible to create very different color paths by manipulating the timing of the color elements. For the dimmed tungsten equipment, you could delay the up-fade time of the yellow light or increase the time that it takes to fade out the blue light. With the color-mixing lights, you could write one or more transitional cues at points along the fade to control how the color path looks. It is important to realize that the more color elements you add into this mix the more complicated the possibilities become!

Besides using our eyes and a trial-and-error approach to manipulating a color path with discrete element timings, is it possible that a path could be calculated for us? How would this calculation work? The simple fade manipulates the color elements, but it does not take into account the luminosity at each point in the path. Remember, with LEDs, this luminosity is no longer a function of saturation. Therefore, especially with LED lights, it's possible to have a nonlinear luminosity output during a color fade, even when the channel level remains constant! This is a problem, and one that we will need computer help to solve.

COLOR PATHS MAKE UNDERSTANDING THE CIE COLOR SPACES RELEVANT

The reason CIE color spaces were developed was and is to try to find a mathematical model that describes what we are experiencing when we look at color. The work of the CIE has been to create a measurable space that attempts to align with how we perceive color. The measurement of the space, and knowing how to plot actual colors within the space, becomes very important because instead of choosing filters to put in front of a light, we are using computers to mix colors in a fixture. And because the multi-emitter LED fixtures have reached a threshold that is now becoming acceptable for general use, we will want to manipulate the color path in every cue. We need to do so because the default approach—where emitters are manipulated linearly from one cue to another without regard to the path—will yield unwanted results. And the math that exists behind the measurable CIE color spaces makes it possible to calculate and manipulate these color paths.

COLOR PATHS TO CONSIDER

Here are some common color path choices that you might want to try when fading from one color to another:

1. Simulate a cross-fade between one unit and another (linear).
2. Maintain saturation across the path (avoid white).
3. Avoid green (skew a path away from green).
4. Avoid magenta.
5. Maintain apparent luminosity across the color path, taking into account the luminosity function.

Each of these path types is calculable within a measurable color space, and the lighting control computer developers are beginning to add this capability. As artists, while it may not be important to understand the math behind these calculations, it is important for us to understand the concept and how this choice of path can radically change how a transition looks.

Let us consider each of these paths in more detail, thinking of a transition between the complementary colors blue and yellow:

1. *Cross-fade simulation.* Back in Chapter 6 (Additive Color Mixing Revisited) we saw the result of transitioning between two lights cross-fading. Mathematically, in a CIE color space, this transition looks like a straight line between the two color points.
2. *Maintain saturation.* Imagine that you want to maintain the saturation between the near spectral colors blue and yellow. The way to do this is to move along the perimeter of the space. This path could also be called "Avoid white."
3. *Avoid green.* Look at the space between blue and yellow in the color space. Skew the path away from green (toward the magenta side of the space).
4. *Avoid magenta.* Look at the space between blue and yellow in the color space. Skew the path away from magenta (up toward the green side of the space).
5. *Manipulate the output intensity* of the color to take into account the luminosity function along the path of transition.

With control technology that was built for subtractive color-mixing systems—before the advent of controllable color paths—trying to manipulate lighting color in this way was often a frustrating experience involving interim cues and specialized timing for the movement of each color flag or emitter.

CONCLUSION

The way a scene transitions from one color state to another can be a storytelling element. We have always sought to control how these transitions worked, but the tools that we had were indirect in that we could only control the timing of a fade. The result was hit or miss, and often many edits in timing were necessary to push a fade into a desired color path. We could not accurately pre-plan a fade within a representation of the color space. Nor could we manipulate the result of a color transition through any means but timing of the discrete color elements.

The ability to directly manipulate the pathway a luminaire takes when transitioning from one color to another is dependent on an accurately measurable color space. The CIE color spaces are attempts to both plot colors in spaces that are measurable and conform to the way most of us see color.

PRACTICAL: MANIPULATING COLOR PATHS BY HAND

Set up four lights in your light lab colored to conform to the three primary colors plus one for amber, all pointing from the same direction to the same area of the cyclorama. Build five sets of transitions or cue sequences using only timing to move the resulting color from blue to yellow that attempt to follow the five pathways outlined in this chapter.

17.

METAMERISM: DEVELOPING A NEW LANGUAGE OF COLOR

AH, THE GOOD OLD DAYS

Before the advent of color-changing luminaires, a production would have one lighting color palette. Now just one verse of a song can have a color palette! The process of choosing colors happened prior to the work in the theater: If you wanted to have a system of lights in Roscolux 68, you asked the producer to purchase X number of sheets of Roscolux 68 and you put that in front of your lights.

In the beginning, color-mixing luminaires were three-color systems. Cyan, magenta, and amber flags were employed to variably filter the white source to arrive at a version of the color. Even though it might not have been a perfect match, with a three-color-mixing system there was usually only one setting to achieve the best match for a given color at a given intensity.

THE INTRODUCTION OF METAMERS

When two colors appear to be the same but are achieved through different means or different recipes, they are considered to be *metamers* of each other.

When more than three color variables exist within a fixture, the possibility arises that there are multiple solutions to match a given resultant color. Think about a moving light with cyan, magenta, amber, and CTO (Color Temperature Orange) filter flags. To arrive at a given pale amber color, you could use either the amber flag or the CTO flag or some combination of both. Any of several color recipes could arrive at the visually equivalent color.

Any time there are more than three colors in a color-mixing system, there will be multiple ways to arrive at a visually equivalent match for some colors.

BUT WE ALREADY KNOW ABOUT THIS...

Since the very beginning of electric stage lighting, we have had systems of lights colored in primary colors with the intention of mixing those primaries to create other colors. My high school, much like many vaudeville theaters, had a set of border lights over the stage with red, green, and blue roundels in them. We used those border lights to create different-colored lighting by mixing the relative intensities of the primary colors.

Still today, we often color cyclorama lighting in the same way. As we have seen, it is possible to create amber light by additively mixing red and green lights onto a surface; it is also possible to use just one light with amber gel to achieve the same effect. If the amber color is the same to your eye whether it is created by mixing a red source with a green source or by turning on an amber source, those two formulas for creating the amber cyclorama can be considered metamers of each other, or two ways to achieve the same result.

BUT WHY IS THIS SO?

Remember, we are trichromats. We have three different types of color detectors in our eyes, and by analyzing the relative stimulation of these three discrete inputs, our brain arrives at an estimation of the color being observed. Because most of us do not have a discrete amber-detecting cone, we actually cannot tell the difference when a) a light that is amber stimulates our red and green cones in a certain way, or b) two lights that are red and green stimulate our red and green cones in exactly the same way. Our vision system can be tricked! Being trichromatic leads to the existence of color metamers.

LED FIXTURES MAKE THIS IMPORTANT

LED fixtures that contain more than three types of color emitters will also be able to produce more than one version of a given color. And by increasing the number of emitter colors in a luminaire, you increase the number of possible metamers for any given color. If you are in the business of matching a gel color with an LED fixture, there are suddenly many more ways to achieve a resulting match.

Metamers are tricky business. What may appear to be a match for a color on a white surface may be quite different when seen on a colored surface. So, with these kinds of fixtures there is the possibility that color can be manipulated in a new way, allowing you to mix colors that look the same on some surfaces and look very different on others. This can be useful to correct for a local costume or scenic color, or it could be used for story-telling purposes.

Today's console software is beginning to help manage metamers, though the polychromatic LED luminaires are sufficiently new enough that we are only beginning to have effective control over metamers. It is important to understand that there can be several recipes for every color when using any color-mixing system with more than three components. Even without sophisticated software help, it is possible to look at a color of light, see the effect it is creating, and try to analyze its component color parts. If you can figure out that the missing component color is a little indigo or that the problem is that the mixed color has too much pale green in it, you will be able to solve the color problem by changing the relative emitter levels manually.

TOWARD A FUTURE SOLUTION

At the moment, our consoles are often challenged with the problem of creating even one accurate match for a given color. But this function has now become not a luxury but a necessity. With the widespread adoption of LED equipment, console software will need to be able to arrive at all the possible metamers for any given color and be able to quickly offer the various choices to the user. However, even if the consoles are technically perfect, it will still be up to you, the designer, to be able to look at a color's component parts and make choices to arrive at your desired color solution.

REMEMBERING YOUR COLORS

Most professional lighting designers who have trained in the use of color filters have memorized the colors that they rely upon from the gel books. With color-mixing systems, this is more difficult. I simply cannot remember that the blue that I liked in that production of *The Tempest* was created by 38% cyan, 22% magenta, and 4% amber, let alone the numbers from a seven-color mixing system! To solve this, I record the component levels of colors that I like in a database, so that I can refer to them in the future and get back to them.

Appendix B is a form that you can use to keep track of all of this color data. Your color names don't have to correspond to a gel color—they could be something personal to you such as "beautiful moonlight" or "angry amber." The important thing is to have a system so you can refer to the colors you like and get them programmed quickly and efficiently.

> *Tip:* *When recording an LED color that you like or that helped to solve a specific problem, write down the local colors of the costumes or scenery for which the color was created. Maybe this is the blue backlight that worked for the fluorescent orange costumes, or for the cornflower blue dress. By understanding the relative values of the emitters, you may better understand why it worked. When you have time, try to find alternate metamers for the colors that you have arrived at for a scene that may help to enhance some part of the overall composition in a good way. Especially experiment with the indigo and lime-green emitter levels within a color.*

PRACTICAL: WORKING WITH METAMERS

Set up a tungsten-based light to project a beam onto a white wall. Set up a Source Four LED-type spotlight so that it projects onto the same wall next to the incandescent light. Put Roscolux 83 into the tungsten light. Match the color of the LED to the tungsten light and record the resulting levels of each emitter type. Then use a different combination of emitter levels to make another match to the gel-colored light. Record those results. How many different combinations of the emitters can you come up with that are close matches to the tungsten light with the color?

Once you have a set of metamers, change the projection surface so that you are projecting the two lights onto a black dyed fabric. Look at each of the previously recorded metamers. How is the match working now for each combination that you are projecting onto the black fabric?

Try the same test with a multicolored fabric. How do the colors in the fabric respond to the gelled tungsten light versus the various metamers of the LED fixture?

18.

CREATING WORK THAT CAN BE REPRODUCED

My work in dance and opera is intended to have a future life, and more often than not, when it moves or is remounted, the equipment will not be the same as what was used in the first iteration. Therefore, my designs must in some way be equipment-agnostic. The design idea must be able to survive changes in the component parts. And this creates a special problem, one that is growing along with the adoption of color-mixing equipment across the industry.

Gel numbers concretely communicate ideas about subtle variations in color and today allow this kind of reproduction and touring. As we transition to a world without actual color media, will the gel numbers continue to be learned and internalized by designers and electricians as they have been?

Imagine our conversations about color when we no longer have a commonly understood color reference such as Roscolux 80. In a fully LED world, these conversations will be very different than they are now, but perhaps they will revert to the more natural language of color that we have talked about in this book: more saturated, less saturated, more dominant, cooler, warmer, etc.

The collective stability of lamps, spotlights, dimmers, and filters has been enormously important in the development and expansion of the theater lighting industry through the 20th and 21st centuries. We have been able to develop a language of lighting so that we can talk about, teach, learn, and collectively explore something as ethereal and immaterial as light.

Additionally, this stability has allowed us to communicate the essence of a design through a set of relatively simple paper-work. With all the variations in equipment manufacture and voltage that exist, a lighting design can be implemented almost anywhere in the world because of the stability and availability of color media and the relatively standardized designs of theatrical lighting equipment.

DIMMER LEVELS AND OUR UNDERSTANDING OF COLOR

LEDs open up many new possibilities for lighting artists. In Chapter 12, on full spectrum and limited spectrum sources, I wrote about re-creating historic or earlier designs. This potentially becomes more and more difficult as we move away from the tungsten sources on which these designs were built. Here is an example: An LED spotlight can currently be made to reliably simulate the light from an unfiltered tungsten spotlight. The same LED fixture can also simulate the color from a tungsten-based spotlight with Roscolux 83 gel—a deep blue color filter. However, because the LED fixture creates colors additively, the total light output of such a source is not related to the saturation of the color as it is with a filtered source. It is quite possible that a given LED fixture creating a simulation of the tungsten white is less bright than the tungsten fixture it is simulating. But when the same LED-based source is set to simulate Roscolux 83, the LED fixture is actually brighter than the equivalent tungsten fixture with the filter.

This large swing in brightness is an inherent feature of LED sources, and it is wonderful that we can now have bright deep colors from a theatrical spotlight. But this means that recorded levels from work that was created with tungsten gear no longer have direct meanings that relate to the LED fixture. Since there is no equivalent mark of "brightness" in an additive fixture to a lamp-based fixture, even a cue made with one kind of LED equipment is very difficult to reproduce with another type of LED gear.

We can experience a pretty faithful version of an original Jean Rosenthal lighting design—even though the luminaires are different and the control technology is different—because there has been a continuity in the method of coloring tungsten sources with subtractive color filters. That even holds true to some extent when transitioning from a tungsten source to an arc source. Since both are colored through subtractive mixing systems, we instinctively understand that deeper colors will not output as much light as paler colors.

Additive mixing luminaires invert the relationship between lumen intensity and color saturation. Our documentation methods need to be revised for designs that will have long lives and reproduced in future season.

Until now it has been possible to reconstruct the designs of the past with relative ease. When we read the 1970s-era lighting plots of Nicola Cernovich, we can both visualize the result and literally reconstruct it in a theater with reasonable success. In fact, this is commonly done, mostly by the dance and opera repertory companies.

On any given night at the New York City Ballet or the Alvin Ailey American Dance Theater, you can see good versions of lighting designs that were created in the 1960s. This becomes more difficult as we move away from lamp-based fixtures and subtractive filters.

I'm not saying this is all bad. Think of all of the new tools that are available to us. The explosion of hardware and software has made it possible to construct extremely precise and detailed designs quickly with the expectation of long-term repeatability in a way that is surely unprecedented in our modern world. But it is rare that we have the time to work with these new tools outside the pressure of a given project's technical rehearsal.

STABILITY IN OUR WORK MEANS THE ABILITY TO RE-CREATE IT

In dance theater, repertory companies are the living repositories of dances and designs from earlier times.

In 2012, I was hired to work with Paris Opera Ballet for their US tour. One of the pieces they were touring, *Giselle*, had scenery that had been meticulously copied and painted from the original 1841 sets. Experiencing that beautiful production is how I imagine it would be to travel back in time. There before us onstage was something that a group of people saw the same way 170 years ago.

Several years ago, my good friend Beverly Emmons was hired as the lighting director and resident lighting designer of the Martha Graham Dance Company. In the years since the ballets had their premieres (with original lighting by Jean Rosenthal), through the intercession of various rehearsal directors, lighting directors, and Graham herself the lighting had morphed away from Rosenthal's original designs.

Emmons took on the task of looking at the original designs with the idea of restoring them as much as possible. To accomplish this, she re-created Rosenthal's original light plots exactly using equipment, lamp types, and wattages that were close to the original specifications. Then Emmons programmed the cues from Rosenthal's original paperwork.

The resulting work was amazing to see. Like the experience of the Paris Opera Ballet's *Giselle*, seeing the Graham Company in rehearsal under those lighting conditions was a revelation. Much less bright than is usual today of course, but such coherence in design and color thinking!

It was a privilege to witness this museum-quality re-creation. And then Emmons used this information to inform her choices in carrying the designs and illumination levels faithfully into modern equipment. Lighting is an art form that, like choreography or costumes or scenery, can and should be preserved.

CONCLUSION

When a dance company tours today, it is usual for a lighting supervisor to re-create as best as possible the original designs using the local lighting equipment. A dance tour does not usually involve trucking, since the scenic demands as well as the financial commitment are less than touring a Broadway show. There are usually only one or two presentations in any given city, and especially since the advent of air travel, a hop around the world for a single or limited number of engagements is not uncommon.

Many dance companies travel with booms for sidelight or they carry equipment while touring within a given country. But in general, because the dance companies use local equipment, the designs are recorded and kept in a set of paperwork (pioneered by Rosenthal and others) that describes the lighting setup (plot and hookup) as well as each state or look of lighting through the course of the ballet (cue list, track sheet, and concept paperwork). Like a wall drawing by Sol LeWitt, the lighting art that we see onstage is maintained and transmitted by this set of instructions. And while the methodology of creating these various forms of paperwork has been computerized over the years, the essence and nature of the instructions has remained in these stable forms, making Emmons's re-creations of Rosenthal's original vision possible.

19.

CONCLUSION: WHERE WE ARE GOING

"We shall not cease from exploration / And the end of all our exploring / Will be to arrive where we started / And know the place for the first time."

—T. S. Eliot, "Little Gidding"

When a successful technology becomes mature, it is often destined to become invisible. I can see a future when this will be true for lighting color technology, though at the moment we are far from that time.

What is an invisible technology? What would it look like for light and color control? Lighting color technology would approach invisibility when the controls to manipulate it were accurate and fixture-independent, without the designer necessarily needing an understanding of the underlying technology from an engineering standpoint. The interfaces to control these fixtures would be commonplace and free of non-artistic jargon. As we move toward greater ease and facility in lighting color manipulation, we start to see the development of the kinds of tools that make the underlying technology less and less visible.

As convenient as the technical jargon of lighting color has been for the documentation and transmission of ideas within the world of professional lighting designers, programmers, and electricians, it has also been a language that separates us from our colleagues who are working with color in scenery and costumes. As a professional lighting designer, I may have discovered that I could solve a particular costume color problem by changing a deep blue light from Roscolux 79 to Roscolux 80, but it is difficult to talk to the costume designer about this solution, because she probably does not share my understanding of the subtle differences in the color signatures (or, more properly, the spectral energy distribution curves) of these two filters. A more direct and time-honored approach would be to engage with the costume designer about how I intend to shift the blue light toward green and away from red, thus translating the technological jargon into more generally understood artistic descriptions for purposes of clear communication.

I think we do this all the time as designers: engage with our colleagues at the necessary level of technical jargon. In many ways, part of our job is to translate jargon into terms that are more universally understood, and vice versa. We are seeing that lighting consoles are starting to be engineered to work with a more universal understanding of how humans see color. As the jargon begins to fall away, our programmers and electricians and consoles are coming back to a language of color that visual artists have always been comfortable with: more saturated versus less saturated, warmer versus cooler, redder versus greener. These ways of talking about color transcend technology and speak directly to the human response to color.

WHERE WE CAME FROM

Colored transparent or translucent filters for stage lighting predate even the electric lamp. Prior to electric lighting, candlelight and gaslight were filtered through colored silks, colored water, and even wine. Later gelatin, high-heat plastics, and finally metal-coated dichroic glass were developed and marketed, with numbering systems that became de facto standards.

The filters that we now use have enjoyed an unprecedented stability over decades of worldwide use, and the trade name numbers of many of the filters have become the common way of speaking about color among lighting professionals. Brigham colored transparent gelatin sheets were brought to market in the 1870s. Plastics, introduced after World War II, could better withstand the heat of stage lights. The method of choosing colors from a swatch book of filter samples in one's studio remained consistent for more than 100 years.

Adding further stability, the majority of Lee brand filters in the 100 series gained their numbers from Cinemoid, a line of color filters that was introduced in the 1960s by Strand. We've had almost 60 years of stable *numbering* in color filters, and generations of designers and technicians and programmers have memorized and internalized these numbers. The lighting industry—engineers, electricians, salespeople, manufacturers, and designers—shares a precise understanding of color because of the worldwide ubiquity of these numbering systems.

A CRISIS OF DOCUMENTATION

The abandonment of this way of talking about color is causing a crisis of documentation. Our work, especially in dance and opera, is often intended to have a future life after an initial run of performances. With especially important works—ballets by

Martha Graham or George Balanchine, for instance—the future life of the original lighting designs has been measured in decades. Often when an opera or ballet moves or is re-mounted, the equipment may not be the same as when it was first created, and the design ideas must be equipment independent. This worked in the past because, while there are many different manufacturers of ellipsoidal spotlights, as an example, the lamp types were similar enough and there was also the stable and consistent worldwide market for stable color filters.

When we live in a post-filter, post-tungsten world, how will this work? How will we describe the color that a particular luminaire output at a particular moment in a show so that it can be reproduced by a ballet company halfway around the world 15 or 20 years from now with some measure of fidelity? We are only at the beginning of finding solutions to this problem, because the technology does not yet exist to *programmatically* re-create all the nuances of a color created with one particular lighting technology with another technology.

I believe that someday we will at least approach a somewhat acceptable level of fidelity. For now, what we can do is record the exact emitter or color flag levels for color mixing luminaires, and we can give that recipe a name that *perhaps* references a filter number, or some poetic name. We don't yet have an automated way to reliably produce that color in another manufacturer's luminaire, or even the next version of the luminaire from the same manufacturer. We don't yet have a way to start with a color mixed on an LED color-mixing luminaire and have a computer system help us find a close matching filter to produce a similar color in a tungsten lamp, or to move reliably from one kind of LED fixture to another that has different component emitters. This is an unsustainable situation in the long-term.

A WAY FORWARD

As LED technology takes over more and more, we are losing the ubiquity of color notation that we have enjoyed, as embodied in the filter numbers and tungsten lights and dimmers. The solution to this dilemma is to look at lighting color independently from the technology of its creation and record the actual spectral power distribution (or SPD) output of the programmed color. Though it may be outside the financial reach of most individual designers today, we are moving to a time when high-quality color meters will become necessary tools for documentation.

Beverly Emmons, along with Steve Terry of ETC, created a project to do exactly this with high-end metering equipment. They documented the SPDs of legacy lighting instruments and filters, powered by direct-current (DC) dimmer technology, so that the early lighting designs of the mid-20th century can be reproduced and studied in the future. In a fast-moving and -developing technological environment, this project points us toward a way forward. We are only beginning to have software tools that can use this data to produce color programmatically, and these tools will have to be developed and refined in order to preserve the design work that is being made today and in the future.

A RETURN TO THE BEGINNING

Many companies across the spectrum of manufacturing industries are moving away from the idea of carving away at materials and leaving waste and moving toward an idea of assembling the exactly correct amount of the right materials to create a product. The shift away from subtractive color, using filters, toward additive color mixing with emitters is an equivalent change in the world of lighting design. There is no possibility of stopping this trend away from tungsten toward LEDs. The reduced power consumption alone dictates it, but as designers we are also drawn to the technology because of all of the new possibilities for color manipulation and switching speed, and the availability of new form factors that this technology brings.

It is important to remember, though, that this technological change doesn't alter the reasons we reach for color as a tool in the first place. Color's connections to time and geographical place, and one's internal sense of these connections, are deeply tied to the human experience. If it wasn't apparent before, LED-based color-mixing luminaires remind us explicitly that there is no such thing as a universal white point and that the color of the light in a scene is *always* a choice. Remember the four reasons why we may consider color in a design:

- for storytelling
- for style
- in the service of scenery, costume, and other color choices in the total visual work, such as projections or the hair color of a particular performer
- as a tool for rendering spatial dimension

None of these reasons is altered by the possible underlying technology of creating the light, whether from an LED, tungsten, or an arc source. What is changing and developing is that as lighting technologies are abandoned, they come to define a period of time. Few people alive today use gaslight to illuminate their homes. Were one to use the *color* and other qualities of gaslight in a lighting design today, she would *necessarily* be making some kind of statement about the time period when gaslight was in general use. As the general use of tungsten, fluorescent, sodium vapor, and other lighting technologies is abandoned, this will be true for them as well. The color and qualities of these kinds of light are fast becoming tools through which we can talk about time periods and style to an audience that may still recognize those specific qualities. This is one way that lighting color by itself can be tied to a period of time.

No matter the technology in use, as lighting designers and artists, color is an extremely important tool in our kit. Unchanging through this time of transition is the quality of sunlight and moonlight and firelight. Unchanging is our vastly complex vision system, whereby photons are turned into chemical and then electrical responses, to become mental pictures and memories that can trigger feelings, ideas, and emotions in the mind of the viewer. Unchanging is the role that lighting color plays in rendering depth in our vision systems. Unchanging is the role that color can play in giving a viewer joy at its mere presence. Celebrate these things and explore the infinite possibilities of color in your own work.

DESIGN FOR A LIGHTING LAB

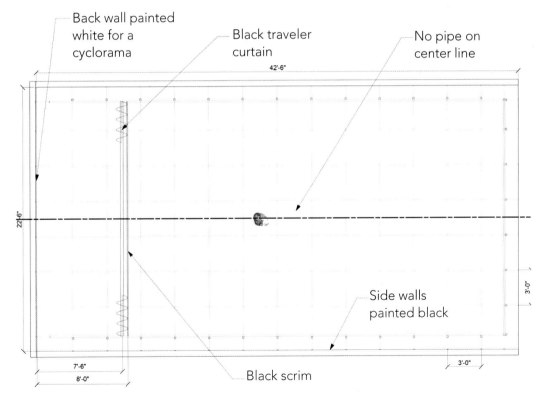

Illus. A.1. Plan for a lighting lab.

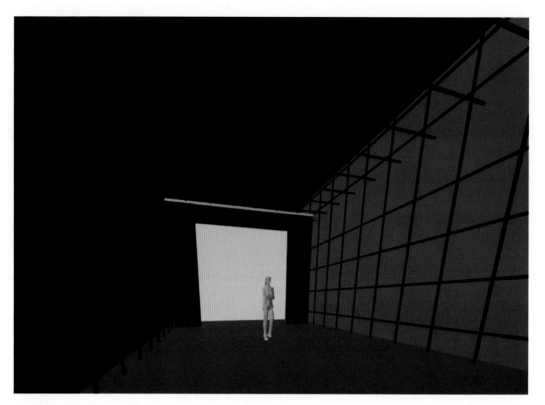

Illus. A.2. Rendering of the lighting lab.

EQUIPMENT LIST

1. A minimum of 8–10 tungsten ellipsoidal lights: The lenses can range in degree, but it is important to have a group of each type so that direct comparisons can be made. For a room of the plan's dimensions, I would suggest that you get six 36-degree, two 50-degree, and two 26-degree lights. In this situation, I think it would also be fine to use zoom ellipsoidals, though in my practice as a working theatrical designer in the United States, I tend to discourage their general use.

2. Twelve PAR lamps: Four Medium Flood, four Wide Flood, and four Narrow Spot 1000w or Source Four replacements.
3. Asymmetric floodlights: At least 18 separate single-cell units that can be placed on the floor or on a pipe overhead.
4. LED color-mixing cyc equipment: I recommend the Selador system because the color space is so large and because their digital dimming system is the smoothest that I have seen. But it is also the most expensive equipment available.
5. Two HMI Fresnels and/or moving light wash sources.
6. Twelve LED ellipsoidal sources.
7. A set of fluorescent tubes of various color types, preferably dimmable.
8. Incandescent "A" lamps in frosted and clear, as well as Edison-type carbon filament bulbs.

And as many of the following sources as you can acquire:

9. A sodium vapor streetlight or factory work light and its associated ballast.
10. A mercury vapor streetlight or factory work light and its associated ballast.
11. A small (short throw) xenon follow spot.
12. LED equipment from as many manufacturers as is practical: Each source is surprisingly different, and the more sources you have the better prepared you will be for using them in your work.
13. Moving light equipment from different manufacturers: Again, each type of unit has different capabilities and different color-mixing engines, so try to obtain as many different types as possible, both currently available and no-longer-made varieties.

14. CXI-type mixing scrollers from Wybron, M-Fader- and S-Fader-type scrollers from Morpheus, SeaChanger color-changing ellipsoidal accessories from Ocean Optics, and Nexera Luminaires from Wybron. Some of these color-changing units are no longer manufactured but are still available on the used-lighting market; they are still in both rental inventory stock as well as many house inventories of equipment in theaters around the world and remain an important tool at this writing.

APPENDIX B:

A FORM FOR RECORDING MIXED COLORS

FIXTURE NAME:

Color Name	Show	Note	1	2	3	4	5	6	7

GLOSSARY

A

A: A standard CIE illuminant representing incandescent or tungsten sources. A is measured at 2856 K.

Additive color mixing: The process of having two or more sources of light from the same direction focused on the same object with two different colors. These colors mix in the viewer's eye after being reflected off the object.

Arc source light: A light source whose light is produced by exciting a sealed container of gas with an arc of electricity.

Asymmetric floodlight: An open-faced light with a lamp and a J-shaped reflector designed to spread light evenly across a flat plane. The lamp is placed within the inner curved space of the reflector. Because the reflector is not round and the lamp is placed on one end of the fixture, it is termed asymmetric.

B

Black body emitter: An idealized mass of material that absorbs all electromagnetic radiation, regardless of frequency. When a black body is raised to a particular temperature, it emits electromagnetic radiation, some of which is visible as light. The color of this visible light is correlated to the temperature (in centigrade) of the emitter plus an offset of 273.15°. For instance, when a black body emitter is raised to a temperature of 2926.85° C (Celsius or centigrade), it will emit a light that is similar to the light emitted from a 3200 K (Kelvin) tungsten lamp.

Brigham: A now discontinued line of color media that were the first standardized color media used on Broadway. The company introduced its line of gels in the 1870s.

C

C: A standard CIE illuminant that represents the color of the northern sky. C Illuminant is 6774 K.

Carbon filament: Thomas Edison's original choice for the filament inside an electric bulb. Carbon was later generally replaced by other materials, most commonly tungsten. However, carbon filament bulbs are still available commercially. The light from a carbon filament lamp is very warm compared with that of a modern incandescent lamp.

Celsius or centigrade degrees: A system of measuring temperature that is calibrated by the changing states of water. Zero degrees Celsius is the temperature at which water freezes, and 100°C is the point at which water boils.

Chocolate color filter: A color filter that combines in one piece of plastic neutral density (gray) and amber filters. A chocolate filter reduces the overall light output of a fixture and also cuts out some cooler wavelengths like purple, blue, and green.

CIE or **Commission Internationale de l'Éclairage (International Commission on Illumination):** The international body that is charged with standardizing the measurements and language we use to talk about and measure light. The CIE has been responsible for publishing the standard representations of color spaces that are used throughout the world today.

Cinemoid: An acetate color medium originally manufactured by Strand.

Color filter: A plastic or glass filter that limits certain wavelengths of light from passing. There are several types of plastic and coating technologies in use. Modern color filters have been developed to withstand the high heat of a high-output luminaire.

Color space: A representation of all the colors that are possible within a given set of constraints. For instance, one could produce a color space for a computer monitor that would show all of the colors that the monitor could display. Color spaces are three-dimensional, though there can be two-dimensional representations of them that are actually sectional slices through the larger three-dimensional space.

Color wheel: An artistic representation of the visible spectrum in which the two extreme ends of the spectrum are joined and the lines of spectral frequencies or colors are formed into a circle or wheel. This simplified way to imagine the spectrum can be useful because it a) acts as a mnemonic device, and b) facilitates the understanding of the relationships between primary, secondary, and tertiary colors.

Complementary colors: This term refers to two colors that are on opposite sides of the color wheel. In a CIE color space, complementary pairs are those whose connecting line passes through the white point. Two examples of complementary colors in light are amber and blue, and green and magenta. If one color in a complement pair is a primary color, then the other color will be a secondary color.

Cone cell: The cells within the eye that detect color. Each type of cone cell can detect one range of color wavelengths. It is thought that our brains perceive color by analyzing the relative intensity of the detection signals of the three different cone cell types.

CRI or **Color rendering index** or **Color rendition index:** The measure of the degree of color shift a defined set of objects undergoes when comparing their color when illuminated by the light source in question to the color of those same objects when illuminated by a reference source of comparable correlated color temperature. (Source: IES *Design Guide for Color and Illumination*, IES-DG-1-16.) CRI is an outdated methodology; TM-30-15 is the current preferred methodology for comparing color rendition in a given white light luminaire.

CTB and **CTO:** Abbreviations for *color temperature blue* and *color temperature orange*. Normally used in the names of color filters used to alter the white point of a lighting source.

Cue: A recorded state of lighting that describes all of the dimmer levels and other control information that can be manipulated, like color or beam parameters on a moving light. In the theater, cues are saved so that they can be triggered in the order of the show. Cues also can contain timing information to record the amount of time that it should take to change from one state of lighting to another.

CXI: (A trademark of Wybron Inc.) A two-scroll subtractive mixing device that uses color filters to achieve a wide range of colors.

D

D50–D75: Standard CIE daylight illuminants. The number after the "D" refers to the Kelvin temperature (D50 is 5000 K).

Dichroic color filter: A glass (or sometimes plastic) color filter that acts not by absorbing the filtered colors but by reflecting them. Because dichroic filters do not absorb the unwanted frequencies, they stay cooler and enjoy a longer life span than other types of filters.

Dichromacy: A vision system that can detect two distinct colors. In humans, this is a defect in which one type of color detection cone is not present. Many animals (especially nocturnal mammals) are dichromats.

E

Edison, Thomas: (1847–1931) The inventor of the electric light bulb and many other marvels of the 20th century.

Ellipsoidal reflector spotlight or **ERS** or **Leko:** A spotlight that outputs a controlled cone of light that can be manipulated to have very sharp edges. The ellipsoidal has developed into the standard theatrical luminaire. It is capable of projecting images that are placed within the beam of light at a certain place within the luminaire. "Ellipsoidal" refers to the shape of the reflector by which the beams of light from a lamp are redirected to flow in one direction. The light can then be manipulated within the luminaire by shaping shutters, gobos, lenses, and color filters. Modern ellipsoidal lights have interchangeable or variable lenses so that a given light can output a range of conical beams of light.

F

F1–F12: Standard fluorescent CIE illuminants.

Filament: The material in a light bulb or lamp that gets heated to produce light. Modern lamps usually employ tungsten filaments, but other materials are possible.

Fluorescent light: A light source first invented in 1857 (see Wikipedia, "Geissler Tube," June 11, 2012) by Heinrich Geissler, long before the invention of the filament lamp. A fluorescent lamp consists of a glass tube that is coated on the inside with a phosphor that is excited by an ultraviolet light. The ultraviolet light is generated by passing an electric current through mercury vapor trapped in the tube.

Footcandle: A measurement of light. One footcandle equals the total amount of light that emanates from a candle measured at a one-foot distance. A footcandle is equal to 10.764 lux.

Footlights: A row of luminaires set on or recessed in the downstage edge of the stage and pointed upstage to illuminate the scene.

Fresnel spotlight: A simple spotlight that consists of a lamp source and reflector on a movable device. The front of this type of luminaire is fitted with a Fresnel-type lens, named after its inventor, Augustin-Jean Fresnel, 1788–1827 (see Wikipedia, "Augustin-Jean Fresnel," June 11, 2012). While this has itself been the subject of several books, for our purposes it's enough to say that this lens type trades a volume of glass for precision. A Fresnel lens can be made much thinner, and therefore less expensively, than a conventional lens. In theatrical Fresnel spotlights, the movable device allows for manipulation of the beam angle from narrow to wide through a continuous range.

G

Gel: See **Color filter**.

Gobo: A cut-out image that can be inserted into the beam of a spotlight and projected to create an image of the cut-out. A gobo can be made of metal (in which case the projected image is literally cut out from the base), glass, or plastic (both can hold full color images).

H

Halogen lamp: An incandescent tungsten filament lamp with a small amount of halogen gas added to the filament chamber. The addition of halogen has the effect of raising the color temperature and also increasing the usable life of the filament. Halogen lamps can be operated at a higher temperature than other incandescent lamps and can therefore create sources that have very high output.

HID or **High-intensity discharge light:** The family of arc lamps including mercury vapor, metal halide, sodium vapor, and xenon. All HID lamps are powered by an electric arc that is formed across a gas-filled space. HID lamps are highly efficient (light output per power input) when compared with incandescent or fluorescent lamps.

HMI or **Metal halide:** An HID-type arc lamp in which the arc chamber is filled with vaporized mercury and compounds of metal with bromide or iodine (halides). The halides are added to improve the color rendition of the lamp.

Hue: The property of a color that describes the relative location of the most prominent color component in the spectral colors: red, yellow, green, blue, and indigo or purple. For instance, even if a light is pink, it can be said to have a reddish hue, and we can talk about pushing its hue toward or away from blue, green, or yellow. For any given color in a color space, the hue of the color is the point on the edge of the color space (along the visible spectrum) that is on the line that begins at the white point and travels through the given color.

I

Incandesce: The process by which a material emits light when it is heated.

Incandescent light: A lamp that generates light when a filament (a thin wire) in the lamp is heated by passing an electrical current through it.

Interpolation: A mathematical process of determining a new point based on the relative positions of other points in a space.

K

Kelvin temperature: A system of measuring temperature. The Kelvin scale begins with 0° at absolute zero, the temperature at which all movement and vibration ceases. Kelvin degrees are scaled the same as Celsius degrees and can be converted to Celsius temperatures by subtracting 273.15°. When used in a lighting context, a Kelvin temperature refers to the proportion of wavelengths of light (color) from a black body emitter raised to a certain number of degrees Kelvin. *Note:* Kelvin is capitalized when used as an adjective, and lowercase when used as a noun. The official abbreviation is K. So, confusingly, "2856 on the Kelvin scale," "2856 kelvin," and "2856 K" are all correct usage.

L

L*a*b* or **(CIELAB):** A revised CIE color space that attempts to correct for perceptual uniformity in print colors. The creation of CIELAB space was heavily influenced by the Munsell Color System.

LED or **Light-emitting diode:** A semiconductor light source that is available in many colors and output configurations.

Lee Filters: A manufacturer of color filters in common entertainment use.

LEED or **Leadership in Energy and Environmental Design:** A suite of rating systems for the design, construction, and operation of green buildings, homes, and neighborhoods.

Leko: Originally a shortening of the trade name Lekolite. Currently used as another name for an ellipsoidal reflector spotlight.

Lens: A piece of glass that manipulates the angles of light passing through it.

Lighting plot: A visual description (scaled plan drawing, scaled section drawing, and other related drawings and schedules) that provides the production electrician enough information to arrange, power, and electronically control a system of lighting to be used in a show.

Limelight: A type of stage lighting that was used before the adoption of electric lighting. Limelight is a gas light with a flame pointed at a hunk of quicklime (calcium oxide) that glows as a result of the heating. Limelight is not green but rather a warm flamelike color.

Linnebach projector: Named after its inventor, Adolf Linnebach, the Linnebach projector was a device from the early 20th century designed to project the image from a painted glass slide onto a large scenic surface. The projector is an open-faced box that is black on the inside with a clear high-intensity lamp within. A painted glass slide is placed on the open side of the device and the image from the painted slide is projected.

Lumen: A measure of light. Lumens measure the total amount of light from a given source irrespective of the area on which the light falls. The light from a projector is stated in lumens. (See also **Lux** and **Footlight.**)

Luminance: A measure of the intensity of light.

Luminosity functions: This describes the average spectral sensitivity of human visual perception of brightness. The functions are based on a series of subjective judgments that compare two colors of light. The human visual system is not equally sensitive to all colors and this range of sensitivities is described by the functions. There are two luminosity functions: One, the *photopic*, describes the phenomenon in brighter light, and the other, *scotopic*, in dim light.

Lux: A measurement of the intensity of light that passes a given area. One lux is equal to one lumen per square meter (lux = lumen/m2).

M

Mercury vapor light: A high-intensity discharge arc lamp in which the light is produced by an electrical arc run through a pressurized mercury gas.

Metamers: Two or more composite colors that, though comprised of different component colors, appear to be identical in some circumstances (as when projecting on a white surface).

Meter: A unit of measure that is approximately 39 inches, or exactly the length of the path traveled by light in vacuum during a time interval of 1/299,792,458 of a second.

Monochromatic: A group of colors that share the same hue but differ in saturation.

Moonlight: Sunlight that is bounced off the surface of the moon back to Earth.

Moving light: A luminaire whose focus and perhaps other attributes can be controlled remotely through a computer interface.

Munsell Color System: A color space that specifies colors based on three color dimensions: *hue*, *value* (lightness), and *chroma* (color purity). It was created by Professor Albert H. Munsell in the first decade of the 20th century. Munsell colors are as close to perceptually uniform as he could make them.

N

Nanometer (nM): A unit of measurement that is one billionth of a meter.

Neon light: A low pressure arc lamp that uses excited neon to produce light. Neon produces light that is orange-red in color. Different gases produce different colors, and in general parlance these are all called neon lights even if they do not employ neon.

Neutral density: A color filter that blocks a certain percentage of light passing through it. A neutral density filter should not alter the color (or proportion of wavelengths) in the light but only the amount of light.

P

Palette: A limited group of colors that are used in a composition. The term refers to a board that is commonly used by painters to hold small quantities of the colors in use while creating a painting.

PAR lamp: Parabolic aluminized reflector lamp. A PAR lamp is a self-contained spotlight with a source, parabolic reflector, and lens built in. PAR lamps have been widely adopted in the theater because they are inexpensive and simple to maintain. PAR lamps come in several size, wattages, and lens configurations. The most common PAR in general theatrical use is the PAR64, which is available in Very Narrow (VNSP or cp60), Narrow (NSP or cp61), Medium Flood (MFL or cp62), and Wide Flood (WFL or cp95) varieties. (US theaters use lettered designations like VNSP; outside the US, with 220-volt systems, it is more common to refer to the "cp" designations, as in "candlepower.")

Pattern: In a stage lighting context, a pattern refers to a gobo. (See **Gobo**.)

Photon: An elementary particle that is the carrier of the electro-magnetic force, which in a specific bandwidth we perceive as light. As an elementary particle, a photon exhibits wave-particle duality and has aspects of both waves and particles.

Pixel: Short for picture (pix) element (el). One dot in an array of dots that form a display, as in a computer monitor or television screen.

Polychromatic: A composition of color that contains multiple hues.

Preset: A state of lighting that is recorded into computer memory (or previously on paper tracking sheets). Presets are often arranged into the order of a show and called cues.

Primary color: A color of visible light that cannot be arrived at by mixing other colors. The primary colors of light are red, green, and blue. The primary colors exist because our eyes evolved with color cones that can directly respond to red, green, and blue wavelengths. Color detection systems that utilize receptors that respond to different color wavelengths would define primary colors differently.

R

Rayleigh scattering: The interaction between atmospheric molecules and light at the shorter (blue) end of the spectrum that makes the sky appear blue.

Retina: The part of the eye that contains the cone and rod cells that respond to light stimulus.

Rig or **Lighting rig:** Lighting industry jargon for the total of a show's lighting equipment. The lighting rig consists of all the luminaires, rigging pipes, cable, and dimmers for a given show.

Rod cell: The specialized cell in the retina of the eye that detects the intensity of light. There are roughly 90 million rod cells in every human eye.

Roscolux: A line of color media for theatrical lighting use manufactured by Rosco Inc.

Roundel: A round piece of glass that is intended to filter a light. Roundels can be colored or clear, and can have textured or smooth surfaces.

S

Saturation: A measurement of color that describes the relationship of a color to a pure spectral color. A color is said to be more saturated as it approaches the edges of a color space. It is said to be less saturated as it approaches the white point of a color space.

Scale: A measured drawing that is prepared to correspond to real world measurements. A drawing in which 1cm corresponds to 25cm of reality is said to be a 1:25 scaled drawing. Common scales in theatrical use are 1:25, 1:50, 1:24 (in the US and UK usually notated as 1/2" = 1'0"), and 1:48 (usually notated as 1/4" = 1'0").

Secondary colors: The three colors that can be derived by mixing any two primary colors. The secondary colors in light are cyan (a mix of blue and green), magenta (a mix of blue and red) and yellow (a mix of green and red).

SED or **Spectral energy distribution:** A term commonly used to quantify the spectral energy passed through a translucent agent such as water, a lens, or a color filter.

Spectral color: The color of a single wavelength of visible light. Spectral colors are those that exist on the spectrum, i.e., can be derived by refracting a full spectrum white light source.

Sodium vapor light: An arc source lamp that uses charged sodium vapor to create light.

SPD or **Spectral power distribution:** Describes the power emanating from a light source as a function of wavelength. (Source: IES *Design Guide for Color and Illumination*, DG-1-16.)

Split gel: Refers to using parts of the frame area for color media in a theatrical luminaire for more than one color. Split gels are sometimes cut along the diagonal, or sometimes arranged so that one color is in the center of the light and a second color is on the perimeter. Different types of lights produce different color effects with split gel. In an Altman 360Q ellipsoidal reflector spotlight, a diagonal cut gel with two complementary colors could produce color fringing effects, especially when combined with a gobo. In other luminaires, a split gel will have the effect of projecting the additive mixture of the two colors. And in some luminaires, you can see the split colors projected onto the area of the stage as a soft image. These different effects depend upon the optics of the luminaire and the particular focus of the individual unit.

Subtractive color mixing: The process of filtering certain frequencies out of a source of light. We subtractively mix a color when we put one or more color filters onto a white light.

Sunlight: The light that the sun emits. Unfiltered sunlight has a color temperature of 5780 K, though this can be altered by atmospheric conditions.

Symmetric floodlight: An open-faced luminaire with a symmetrically shaped (could be a cylindrical or elliptical section) reflector. The lamp is placed in the center of the curve to maximize the potential of the reflector.

Synaptic response: A description of the process within the brain whereby decisions are made and memories created. The electrical state of the optical nerve causes a synaptic response in the part of the brain that processes visual information.

T

Technical rehearsal: Sometimes called a *lighting rehearsal*, the period in the preparation of a theatrical presentation when the lighting states and changes are created and programmed.

Technicolor: A film process for producing color transparencies for use in the cinema. Technicolor was widely used in Hollywood from the 1930s through the 1950s. It is known for its hypersaturated colors.

Tertiary color: A spectral color that can be derived by mixing a secondary color with an adjacent primary color. The exact location of tertiary colors on the spectrum is subjective. Some examples of tertiary colors are orange (between primary red and secondary amber), violet (between primary blue and secondary magenta), rose (between primary red and secondary magenta) and chartreuse (between primary green and secondary amber).

Tetrachromacy: A vision system that utilizes four types of color detectors, of which the fourth type of rod cell detects amber light directly. Some women have this tetrachromatic mutation. The belief is that this mutation affords the carrier superior skill in detecting changes in skin tone.

TM-30-15: A method for evaluating and reporting light-source color rendition. (Source: IES *Design Guide for Color and Illumination*, DG-1-16.) TM-30-15 was developed to replace CRI as a more robust evaluation of how a white light source renders color.

Tracking sheet: A form for recording all of the dimmer levels for a state of lighting (or a cue) in a show.

Trichromacy: A vision system that utilizes three types of color detectors. Humans are generally trichromatic.

Tungsten filament: The filament in most modern incandescent lamps is made from the element tungsten. This filament heats up and begins to incandesce when an electrical current is passed through it.

U

Ultralume: A Philips-branded fluorescent source designed for retail spaces. It has a color temperature of 3000 K, with a CRI of 85 that is similar to that of illuminant F12.

u'v': A two-dimensional diagram that is a representation of the CIE 1976 L*U*V* color space at a given luminosity. CIE 1976 L*U*V* is a color space adopted by the International Commission on Illumination or Commission Internationale de l'Éclairage (CIE) in 1976, as a transformation of the1931 CIE XYZ color space that attempts perceptual uniformity. It is extensively used for applications such as computer graphics that deal with colored lights.

W

Wavelength: The distance between peaks in a vibrating particle or wave. The wavelengths of visible light are measured in nanometers. Wavelengths are related to the amount of energy that is carried by the particle, in this case a photon.

White point: The CIE measurement of an unfiltered (and idealized) illuminant. A white point is said to have a Kelvin temperature that corresponds to the proportion of wavelengths of light from a black body emitter raised to a certain degree centigrade.

X

Xenon source light: An arc source lamp that uses charged xenon gas to create light.

xyY: The names for the three axes in the 1931 CIE color space. Lowercase X and Y are arbitrary measurements such that every color within the space falls between 0 and 1 on both scales. Uppercase Y refers to luminosity. The colors in the main 1931 chart all have a luminosity of 100.

XYZ: The names of the three axes in the CIE XYZ color space. This is a universal color space, i.e., it is device independent. The three values correspond to the three primary colors of light, with X referring to red, Y referring to green, and Z referring to blue. XYZ values are typically reported by spectrometers. These values can be mapped into other color spaces through mathematical transformations.

REFERENCE AND FURTHER READING

Albers, Josef. *Interaction of Color*. New Haven, CT: Yale University Press, 1975.

Berlin, Brent, and Paul Kay. *Basic Color Terms: Their Universality and Evolution*. Berkeley, CA: University of California Press, 1969.

von Goethe, Johann Wolfgang. *Theory of Colours*, English edition. London: John Murray, 1840.

Itten, Johannes. *The Art of Color*. New York: Van Nostrand Reinhold Co., 1973.

McCandless, Stanley. *A Method of Lighting the Stage,* Fourth edition. New York: Theatre Arts Books, 1958.

Munsell, Albert H. "A Pigment Color System and Notation." *The American Journal of Psychology* 23 (1912). Champaign, IL: University of Illinois Press.

Newton, Isaac. *Opticks: Or a Treatise of the Reflexions, Refractions, Inflexions and Colours of Light.* London, 1704.

Parker, W. Oren, and R. Craig Wolf. *Scene Design and Stage Lighting*, Sixth edition. Chicago: Holt, Rinehart & Winston, 1990.

Rosenthal, Jean, and Lael Wertenbaker. *The Magic of Light: The Craft and Career of Jean Rosenthal, Pioneer in Lighting for the Modern Stage*. Boston: Little Brown & Co., 1972.

Salle, David. *How to See: Looking, Talking, and Thinking About Art*. New York: W.W. Norton & Company, 1986.

Stanley, Mark. *The Color of Light Workbook*. Port Chester, NY: Rosco Laboratories, 1987.

INDEX

91; defined, 202; Kelvin temperature scale loosely plotted onto, *83*; line plotted on between magenta and cyan, *64*; with monochromatic line from blue to white, *118–19*; and more accurate depiction of colors of visible light, *50*; three colors plotted on and swatches for colors at points of triangle, *65*

Cinemoid, 178, 189

color, and culture, xxiii, 15–17; absence of distinction between blue and green in premodern languages, 16; color as subject of cultural research, 16–17; cultural color palettes, 19–20; cultural color preferences, 115; cultural evolution of color words, 17–18; hierarchy of color words across languages, *17–18*, 37; language used to describe colors in different cultures, 16

color, and lighting design: importance of context, 2; manipulation of color through light, xxiii; potential roles of, 2–3; in service of scenery, costume, and performers, 3, 5–6, 8, 181; for storytelling, 3, 8, 181; for style, 3, 4–5, 8, 181; as tool for rendering spatial dimension, 3, 7, 8, 181; and white light, 87

color, as biological response to photonic energy, 11, 15. *See also* vision system

color choices, necessity for, 18–19

color circle: arrangement of primary and secondary colors, *43*; classic, 53; defined, *40, 190*; distance problem, 61–63, *62*; flattened into triangular shape, *45*; magenta in, *40*–41; modern, *41*; Newton's, in Latin, *39*; new version of, *43*; as predictive tools, 45; with primary and secondary color names, *90*; with three complementary pairs, *44*–45; with two line segments of equal length, *61*–62. *See also* color triangle

color diagrams: lack of representation for black, brown, and gray, *51. See also* color circle; color triangle; Commission Internationale de l'Éclairage (aka CIE)

color dominance, 102–17; color effects, and audience's understanding of space, depth, and meaning, *109*; color effects when lighting a figure in three-dimensional space, *108–9*, 110; color hierarchy as function of brain, 106; general guidelines for, 107–8; role in desaturation process, *104–5*; and

subject and field studies in two-dimensional space, 102–6, *103–5*

color fatigue, and saturation, *92–94, 93*, 99

color filter: defined, 189; evolution of, 6–7, 177; stability of over decades, 6, 178; stable numbering of, 7, 178; swatch book of, 6

color mixing, schematic look at, 39–41

color notation, loss of ubiquity of, 180

color palettes: and color perception, 92; cultural, 19–20; custom, 135; defined, 198; pale tinted, 100–101; polychromatic, 120, 121. *See also* monochromatic palettes

color paths: and color-mixing luminaires, 159–60; common choices when fading from one color to another, 161–62; manipulating by hand, 163; plotting accurately from one color to another, 63–65; and relevance of CIE color spaces, 160–61; with same beginning and ending points that travels through white, *55*

color perception: dependence on color palette of composition, 92; relativity of, xxiii–xxiv, *87*, 92; unequal perception of colors, 106

color pigments, history of, 133

198; result of cone cells, 24–26, 29

printer inks, primary colors in, 26

programming color with additive and subtractive systems, 158

Rayleigh scattering, 113–14, 199

recessive colors, and shadows, 110–13

red act curtain, 94

red and green light, colors resulting from mixing, *46*

redshifting effect, 52–53; shifting color filters to compensate for, 144; simulating with LED-sourced luminaires, 145–46, 149; in tungsten/ incandescent fixtures, 143–45, 148

Requiem, Buglisi Dance Theatre, *98–99*

retina, xxiv, 11, 13–15, 25, 27, 28, 94, 199

rig (lighting rig), 199

Robins, Laila, *129*

rod cells: defined, 199; and detection of brightness and darkness, 27

Roscolux, 199

rose, 37, 201

Rosenthal, Jean: *The Magic of Light*, 94; original lighting for Martha Graham Dance Company, 173–74; records of lighting setup, 174–75

roundel, defined, 199

Russell, Paul, lighting for *Farinelli and the King*, 130

Salle, David, *How to See*, 134

saturation, 90–101; and color fatigue, *92–94*, *93*, 99; deep, and illusion of darkness, 98–99; defined, 199; path of, 119; as property of color, 90, 99

Savoy Theatre, London, first use of electric lighting for stage, xx

scale, defined, 199

schematic lighting plot: showing sidelight from either side of figure with color-mixing devices on one side and nonmixing ellipsoidal on the other, *79–80*; showing sidelight from either side of figure with three lights each, *74*

scotopic function, 106–7

scrollers, 150–51

Sea-Changer, 78

secondary colors, 31–33, 37; appear to embody range of color frequencies while remaining saturated, 73; on 1976 CIE chart, *60*–61; cyan, magenta, and yellow on color wheel, *60*; defined, 200; designing lighting compositions using only saturated secondary colors, 73–74; diagram showing

primary colors, additively mixing to secondary colors and white, 35; mix of any two resulting in version of white, 59, 61, 72. *See also* amber; cyan; magenta

"*See* with your eyes," 20

sepia, 132

S-Fader, 78

shadows, and recessive colors, 110–13

skin tones, 155

sky: fill light representing light from, *112–13*; as light source, 110–11

slate, *36*

sodium vapor lighting: defined, 200; limited spectrum source, 83, 127; power efficiency, 128

spectral colors, 30, 36, 200

spectral energy distribution (SED), 200

spectral power distribution (SPD): defined, 200; graph, *125*, 126; recording of for legacy lighting instruments, 180

split gel, defined, 200

stage lighting: blue-to-yellow complementary pair and, *53*; building from back of stage to front, 115; tungsten filament lamp as primary lighting device for, xx

Strand filters, 178

strobing shutters, 148

subtractive color mixing, 32, 75–80; combining two or more filters in a single light, 77–78; defined, 201; and intensity and color as two separate ideas, *152*; with mechanical systems, 78–79; paint, inkjet printers, or color-mixing filter flags, 76; secondary colors becoming primary colors in, 75; in a subtractive (filtered) color arrangement, *76*; three primary colors of cyan, magenta, and yellow, 77

sunlight: an idea of, *111*–12; defined, 201; as full spectrum source, 124–25; at midday, 114

swatch books, 6, *22*, 178

symmetric floodlight, 201

synaptic response, 201

Tagliarino, Sal, 110

Technicolor, defined, 201

technical rehearsal (lighting rehearsal), 201

Technicolor film stock, 17, 132

Terry, Steve, 180

tertiary colors, 35–36, 37, 201. *See also* chartreuse; rose; violet

tetrachromacy, 28, 202

theater lighting industry, importance of stability of lighting technology, xx–xxi, 170–71. *See also* dance and opera; stage lighting

TM-30-15, 85, 127, 202

tracking sheet, 202

trichromacy, 25–26, 166, 202

tungsten filament, defined, 202

tungsten sources: cannot simulate instantaneous color changing or strobing of LED fixtures, 149; lack of power efficiency, 128; mixing with non-tungsten sources, 136; with MSR moving lights, 77, 83; primary lighting devices for stage, xx; spectral components of, *84*; theatrical lights filtered with color media, 135

Turner, J. M. W., *Fishermen at Sea*, 70–*71*

Ultralume, 202

universal colors, English language hierarchy of, 18

u′v′, 202. *See also* CIE 1976 u′v′ Color Space

Vari-Lite 3500 moving light, 134

video projectors, and color integration, 85–86

violet, 23, 31, 35, 201

visible spectrum, 11–12, *13*–15, 47–51

vision system: cone cells, 14–*15*, 24–26, 28, 29, 154, 190; evolved to perceive light not absorbed by atmosphere (optical window), 11–12, 14; experience of color based on light reflected from object into eyes, xxvii, 12–13; optic nerve, xxiv, 15; retina, xxiv, 11, 13–15, 25, 27, 28, 94, 199; rod cells, 27, 199

warm white, 61

wavelength: defined, 203; of photons, 11, 14

white balance, and projection, 85–86

white light: artistic definition and technical definition, 91; can be saturated, 81; colors more dominant than, 137; defined, 12; and Kelvin temperature, 82–83; limited spectrum sources and, 83–85; as mixtures of component colors of light, 10, 81; primary colors mixed to create secondary colors and white light, *33, 42, 44*; variability of perception of, 86–*89*

white point: defined, 203; finding, 87, 120

Wybron CXI, 78, 151

Wybron Nexera, 151

Xenon source light, 203

xyY, 203

XYZ, 203

yellow, as spectral color, 45

yellow-greens, pale, usually most dominant colors in palette, 108